ON FAIRNESS

A systematic analysis of the concept of fairness as a moral notion. The work critically examines and rejects several familiar accounts of fairness - fairness as equality of treatment, as not taking advantage of another, as adherence to rule, and as respect for others - the author proposes an alternative account of fairness as fidelity to social practice.

Drawing on examples from a variety of social practices, ranging from the requirement to do one's fair share to the fairness of lotteries and bargaining, this book outlines a new moral theory of fairness and offers insight into the various roles fairness considerations play in our lives and their limitations. Reflecting on the place of fairness and fairmindedness in moral, social, and political thought, this book will be of interest to moral, social and political philosophers as well as those in related areas such as political science and sociology.

I0888655

ASHGATE NEW CRITICAL THINKING IN PHILOSOPHY

The *Ashgate New Critical Thinking in Philosophy* series aims to bring high quality research monograph publishing back into focus for authors, the international library market, and student, academic and research readers. Headed by an international editorial advisory board of acclaimed scholars from across the philosophical spectrum, this new monograph series presents cutting-edge research from established as well as exciting new authors in the field; spans the breadth of philosophy and related disciplinary and interdisciplinary perspectives; and takes contemporary philosophical research into new directions and debate.

This book is dedicated to my mother
and the memory of my father

On Fairness

CRAIG L. CARR
Portland State University

Routledge
Taylor & Francis Group
LONDON AND NEW YORK

First published 2000 by Ashgate Publishing

Reissued 2018 by Routledge
2 Park Square, Milton Park, Abingdon, Oxon OX14 4RN
711 Third Avenue, New York, NY 10017, USA

Routledge is an imprint of the Taylor & Francis Group, an informa business

A Library of Congress record exists under LC control number: 00131670

ISBN 13: 978-1-138-71241-6 (hbk)
ISBN 13: 978-1-138-71239-3 (pbk)
ISBN 13: 978-1-315-19999-3 (ebk)

Contents

Acknowledgements

This work began as a simple article which just kept growing as friends and colleagues made me painfully aware of the complexity of the subject I had undertaken and of how far short my thoughts fell from doing it justice. Although I suspect that my thoughts still fall short, it is only fair to offer a heartfelt thanks to those influences most responsible for guiding and encouraging their development. I benefitted greatly, and continue to do so, from the helpful comments and thoughtful insights of Mike Seidler and Mike Philips. Nathan Austin, who read the manuscript in its early stages, called my attention to a great many problems that needed to be addressed. I fear I have not met all the challenges he posed to my arguments. Stephen Moore read through the whole manuscript with his characteristic thoroughness and offered invaluable substantive and editorial advice. Along the way I also profited from the dedicated efforts of several graduate assistants. A special thanks to Jennifer Pennell, Lori Kinder, and Gwen Thompson for all the help. And then there is my friend, colleague, and sometimes collaborator Gary Scott, whose advice, encouragement, and support kept me going. Although it may seem somewhat unusual, I also want to thank Jim Cooke, Jim Solberg, and the other "big sticks" at Mt. Park who kept me running and who graciously indulged me as I asked them endless questions about the nuances of fair play. Lastly I must thank Molly Dahms whose expertise made the otherwise trying challenges of manuscript preparation fade away.

Chapter One

Introduction: Dimensions of Fairness

For some reason, the notions of fairness and unfairness have received little studied attention. Rarely if ever do discussions of fairness figure in the classic texts of moral and political thought. Rarely if ever does one find a theoretical work of any sort devoted exclusively or at least largely to understanding what it means to be fair or unfair. Such apparent neglect is even more surprising when one considers the tremendous scholarly attention that has been directed toward the conceptually related notions of justice and equality. Both these notions figure prominently in the classic literature of moral and political discourse. Both have been, and continue to be, the targets of rigorous conceptual analysis, and both are frequently found at the heart of more comprehensive moral and political theories.

This lack of attention might indicate that the concept of fairness is not as fundamental to our moral and political reflections as concepts like justice and equality, and therefore not in need of much discussion or analysis. But this dismissive conclusion hardly seems warranted when we consider the moral importance we ordinarily attach to being fair. Fairness, I think it fair to say, raises significant moral concerns, and claims about being treated unfairly carry considerable moral weight--at least as much, if not more, than claims about being treated unjustly or unequally. Similarly, the need to play fairly, to bargain fairly, or simply to *be* fair matters to individuals of strong moral integrity.

Perhaps, however, the notion of fairness so closely overlaps the more prominent notions of justice and equality that it is pointless to make much of whatever differences of usage might separate them. Brian Barry has warned that, "It is a cardinal error . . . to suppose that merely because there are two words there must be two well-differentiated concepts" (1989: p. 145). No doubt there is a good deal of truth to this. But it would be a cardinal error of a different sort to conclude that notions like justice and fairness are not well-differentiated concepts simply because they are frequently used in similar linguistic contexts and appear at times to overlap in meaning. The thing to do, I suppose, is to look and see if it is possible to discern significant conceptual or normative differences here.

This introduces the purpose of the study to follow--to look and see. I intend to move the notions of fairness and unfairness out from behind the shadow of their more illustrious conceptual cousins and consider them in their own right. This should enable us to recognize the independent role they play in moral discourse and to appreciate the significant normative concerns they introduce. It should also enable us to expose, recognize, and remedy some serious conceptual confusion which continues to surround the notions of fairness and unfairness. Some sense of the confusion I have in mind can be gained by considering a few of the more prominent philosophical accounts of fairness.

A list of these possible accounts, culled from the meager literature on the subject, would most likely include the following:

1. Fairness involves not disadvantaging others.
2. Fairness involves being unbiased, impartial, or neutral in our treatment of others.
3. Fairness involves sharing burdens or benefits equally, or maintaining a proper proportion between benefit and contribution.
4. Fairness involves treating equal or similar cases equally or similarly.
5. Fairness involves adhering to the rules.
6. Fairness involves treating others with the concern and respect they deserve.

Now, this list is suggestive but by no means exhaustive. Additions, however, are likely to involve little more than variations on at least one of the themes expressed by these six accounts. So I will suppose the list offers a reasonably comprehensive view of the various ways in which we might understand what it means to be fair.

Each of these possibilities has a certain intuitive appeal, and it is easy enough to think of situations where they all seem to get something about fairness right. Yet they are also all quite distinct; while there is a good deal of overlap between some of them (e.g., 3 seems a specific instance of 4), they do not simply repeat the same logical territory. Given the confusion created by these differing accounts, we might think that the thing to do is to see which account gets closest to the heart of the notion of fairness. Perhaps some of these accounts are too specific, capturing only one dimension of fairness. If it is possible to discern which of these accounts is properly comprehensive, we might be able to put the list in some type of logical order and gain a better insight into the nature of fairness.

This is one way, and I think a reasonably profitable way, to approach an inquiry into the meaning of fairness. However--and as should be evident--it is entirely possible that none of the accounts on my list provide an adequate account of fairness. In fact, I think this is the case, and so I will have occasion to add to the list. The addition I will recommend involves thinking of fairness--roughly for the moment--in terms of fidelity to social practice.

All this will begin to come into plain view, however, only after we have examined the various accounts of fairness on the list and held them up to critical scrutiny. And this introduces the game plan for what follows. The first four chapters are devoted to a discussion of whether there is anything to be said for the familiar (yet competing) views of fairness listed above. In the process, the notion of fairness as fidelity to social practice will emerge as a promising possibility. I take up this notion in earnest in Chapter Five and work in the remaining chapters to smooth out its rough edges, make it at least reasonably clear, and explore some of its more prominent implications for the nature of fairness as a moral notion. To anticipate the results of the discussion ever so slightly, I will locate fairness within the context of moral concerns that govern the activity of joining with others and pursuing some type of cooperative venture. Fairness, this is to say, matters from a moral point of view because it is a central virtue of cooperation, and we are, of course, social beings who both want and need to cooperate with one another.

The Material and Formal Dimension of Concepts

A few preliminary remarks are necessary to clarify and orient the argument to follow, and these will occupy the remainder of this chapter. The first of these is primarily methodological in character. Trying to get clear on the nature of a concept like fairness gives rise to an immediate problem. It is difficult if not impossible to reflect on the notion of fairness without the aid of examples to illustrate cases of fair or unfair behavior. If there was not general agreement on whether a particular course of conduct was fair or unfair (as well as on whether it makes sense to speak of such conduct as fair or unfair) we could not begin to make sense of fairness. This much is all but trivially true. But once we bring specific examples of, say, unfairness onto center stage, we complicate the problem of analysis.

This is because it is possible to disagree about whether a particular example illustrates unfairness in several ways. Consider, for example, a situation where A, who is playing a game of cards, deals off the bottom of the deck. Imagine that both B and C, who happen to be A's opponents in the game, notice this. They might both infer from their independent observations that A is cheating, and this might incline them both to conclude that A is playing unfairly. But there is room for disagreement here on several fronts. First, they might disagree on whether A is cheating by dealing off the bottom of the deck. (What would we say if A always deals off the bottom of the deck?) But they might also agree on this and still disagree on whether A is playing fairly. In the example at hand, this will seem silly; cheating always seems to be unfair, although we might also be able to imagine circumstances where it is the right thing to do. But there may be other situations where it is less clear whether a particular type of conduct qualifies as unfair.

Let me suppose for the moment that B and C do disagree over whether A is playing fairly, and let me suppose further that they happen to agree that A is cheating. We might now want to say that B and C disagree over the nature of fairness and unfairness. But this is not necessarily so; odd as it may sound, they could agree on the nature of fairness and unfairness and still disagree in their judgments about whether A's cheating qualifies as unfair. The point is of some importance because if we fail to see that we can disagree in judgments about whether specific actions are fair, without disagreeing about the nature of fairness, we may mistakenly conclude that disagreement in such judgments justifies objecting to a particular theoretical account of fairness. But the point is also not intuitively obvious, and so a bit more needs to be said to make things clear.

To begin, I want to enlist the services of a useful distinction introduced some time ago by Julius Kovesi. Kovesi noticed that some of the concepts integral to our normative vocabulary resemble Chinese boxes with more specific notions comprehended by more general ones. What he calls the material element of a concept is given by concrete examples or instances of the concept in question. But these concepts also have a formal element that indicates why some concrete example or instance of a concept is associated with this particular concept and not with a different one (1967: ch. 1). As Kovesi put it,

> We can commit murder in a great variety of ways. It is the material element of an act of murder that someone drives a knife into his victim's heart, or administers poison, or strangles him, or pushes him over a cliff. Human ingenuity may increase this list, and we may never be able to give a complete enumeration of the ways one can murder someone. What makes all these pieces of human behavior into acts of murder is what I call the *form* of murder, i.e. that we intentionally take the life of someone who is innocent, with the aim of personal gain or satisfaction (1967: p. 4; emphasis in original).

In Kovesi's terminology, which I will adopt here, certain concepts have both formal and material elements. The notion of murder, for example, works as a formal notion understandable in terms of the intentional taking of an innocent life. But it is also a material element of the concept of homicide because it involves a particular type of homicide, viz., the intentional and unjustified taking of life for specific reasons. Similarly, murder is also a material element of the notion of moral wrong because it is recognized to be a type of morally unjustified behavior. And so, some concepts slide into more comprehensive ones and become material conditions of larger formal notions, which might, in turn, slide into yet other, more comprehensive notions.[1]

This distinction can help guide linguistic analysis if it is employed to clarify the task at hand. By focusing on a concept's formal element we are able to understand the target of analysis as a particular type of tool or mechanism. This permits us to see and appreciate the kind of work we can do with the concept in question. By focusing on a concept's material element, on the other hand, we can discern how the target of our analysis operates within some specific linguistic context. Taking this as a clue, we might suppose that an adequate theory of fairness should do two things. First, it should provide a reasonably coherent and comprehensive account of the concept's formal element, and second, it should indicate how the concept works as a material element within a larger conceptual context.

It is not always easy to discern a concept's formal element, however, and we might wonder about how to go about doing so. One way to account for this is to say that it is simply a bundle of all those material elements that we happen to associate with the concept in question. To get clear on fairness and unfairness, in this event, we would have to take inventory of the different ways we can be fair or unfair. This may not seem like a terribly profitable approach since material instances of fairness might be open ended in much the way Kovesi supposes the material element of murder to be open ended. But there is a more pressing reason to reject the bundle theory.

Consider again the situation where A deals off the bottom of the deck and both B and C notice this. Imagine B concludes from this that A is playing unfairly and challenges her actions. Suppose, now, that A concedes that she was dealing off the bottom of the deck and that this is a material instance of cheating, but that she does not think her cheating is unfair. In effect, she is raising a question about the meaning of fairness; or rather, she is raising a question about the formal element of fairness and not about exactly what she has done. Her question does not necessarily suggest that she does not think she has acted wrongly; she might concede that cheating is wrong. So we can suppose that her question is not about the moral condemnation carried by B's charge but about the nature of the charge itself. She wants to know why her cheating is an instance of unfairness and not an instance, say, of injustice or something else. The bundle theory cannot provide an answer to this question; it arbitrarily subsumes material instances of unfair actions under the formal element of unfairness.

Kovesi explains why the bundle theory will not work as follows:

> The reasons why we cannot define what a thing or act is in terms of their material elements, or why we cannot make valid deductive arguments where the premisses contain only material elements and the conclusion tells what the thing or act is, is not a special characteristic of evaluative arguments. It has to do with the fact that the sort of things that can constitute a thing or act, their material elements, cannot be enumerated in a final list. It is their formal element which will determine what they are, not a list of their material elements (1967: p. 8).

If the formal element does not power the judgments the notion at issue allows us to make, the material elements would not necessarily be open ended. But of course it is not the open endedness of the material elements that explains why the formal element must determine the nature of the judgments the notion at issue allows.

To understand why the formal element powers our understanding of key notions, it is necessary to examine how this element enables us to make the judgments that we do. As I noted previously, cases of cheating always seem to be unfair, but even here it is possible to raise a key question. Are there occasions when cheating is not unfair? We cannot really answer this question until we have some sense of what fairness and unfairness involve. This is another way of saying that we cannot be certain about what type of conduct will be judged as fair or unfair by looking only at the conduct itself, and this, in turn, indicates that we cannot identify the formal element of a concept by looking for a bundle of its material elements. Nor can we deduce the formal element from a relatively exhaustive list of its material elements. We must first have some inkling of the formal element before we can identify the material elements in question.

So then, a concept's formal element precedes, in a logical sense, its material dimensions. Without the formal element, we simply cannot recognize specific actions as instances of something. Cheating is unfair because of what it means to act unfairly. That is, because we have a sense of unfairness, we can recognize cheating as an instance of unfairness. Our concepts of fairness and unfairness thus empower our ability to judge and to reach certain conclusions about what others have done or how they have behaved.

Yet while a concept's formal element has a certain logical priority in our understanding over its material elements, the search for the formal element seems curiously dependent upon the careful analysis of its material instances. To get clear on the formal element of fairness, then, we need to spend a good deal of time examining what seem to be clear cases of fair and unfair conduct. But disagreement may surround even what I consider to be a relatively straightforward instance of unfairness. This is not necessarily problematic, however; in fact it isn't problematic if it turns out that the disagreement is actually over the material element of fairness and not over my claims about its formal element.

Recall once more the case of A's putative cheating by dealing off the bottom of the deck. I imagined above that B and C are agreed that A is cheating but that they disagree on whether A is playing unfairly, and I said that this disagreement need not indicate that B and C disagree over the nature of fairness. We are now able to make some sense of this. For the disagreement here may be over whether cheating is a material instance of unfairness and not over the formal element of unfairness itself. There is, in principle, at least some room for disagreement in judgment over a concept's material elements since the relation between formal and material elements is not a matter of simple deduction. Suppose, for example, B and C are agreed that fairness involves, say, not taking advantage of others. Suppose, too, that both B and C believe that dealing off the bottom of the deck is a way to cheat by raising one's chances of getting winning cards. Does it follow that by cheating in this way A is taking advantage of B and/or C? If B and C disagree about this, their disagreement will be over whether A is playing fairly, but not over the meaning of fairness.

It follows that raising an objection to a specific example, or claiming that a putative example of unfairness does not really exemplify an unfairness, does not necessarily count as an objection to a particular construction of the formal element of fairness. Things are different, however, if B and C disagree about whether fairness involves taking advantage of others. If B thinks fairness involves not taking advantage of others, and C thinks fairness involves adherence to rule, they may actually agree that A's actions are unfair, even though they happen to disagree on the formal element of fairness. Of course, they would also disagree over whether A's actions are fair if B does not think A's actions take advantage of anyone and if C believes that A's actions violate the rules of play.

It is also worth noting that a concept can have only one formal element. If we find a term with two formal elements, we have one term or word but two concepts. It does not follow, however, that a concept's formal element ultimately or necessarily reduces to a final, simple notion that can be articulated in the form of a reasonably coherent theory. The desire for such parsimony is a feature of theorizing that is not necessarily honored by our linguistic world. We cannot know, prior to theorizing, whether concepts like fairness and unfairness are "amenable" to theoretical scrutiny or whether their subtlety, complexity, and nuance are likely to be sacrificed by any effort to theorize about their formal element. We can only proceed with our analysis and see what comes of it. We may discover something about these concepts that help will us to understand better the nature of our moral and political lives, or we may meet with nothing but confusion, uncertainty, and frustration. We may even affect the way the concepts of fairness and unfairness work for us. Language is subject to dialectical revision; the more we work with language to understand ourselves, the more we affect, for better or worse, who we are.[2]

If being forewarned is to be forearmed, then we should not expect more, in the way of tidiness and simplicity, from a theoretical account of fairness and unfairness than the complexities introduced by these notions will permit. When it comes to something like conceptual analysis, it is not a matter of getting it right--whatever this could mean--but of supplying a vantage point from which to consider the logic of the conceptual tools at our disposal. As speakers of a common language, such theorizing can tell us something, and perhaps something of importance, about ourselves. But it is only as instructive, it is only as provocative, as we think it to be and as we want it to be.

Two Concepts of Fairness

Concepts, we have seen, can have numerous material instances but only one formal element. On the other hand, if we have but one word, it does not follow that we also have only one concept. The word 'fairness', for example, might designate different concepts with different formal elements, and in fact this seems to be the case.

Sometimes claims of fairness are little more than general assertions of commendation or propriety, and similarly, sometimes claims of unfairness involve generic assertions of disapprobation or impropriety. For example, statements exclaiming, "that's fair," could mean something like "that's okay," "that's good," or "that's alright," while statements asserting "that's not fair," or "that's unfair," might express something like, "that's wrong," or "that's not right." In the former case, the claim of fairness asserts the judgment that things are proper or as they should be, and in the latter case, the claim of unfairness conveys the judgment that something has gone wrong or is not as it should be. Often this appeal to fairness or unfairness expresses a person's opinion about something that has affected him or her either positively or negatively. A person unhappy with some outcome may express this unhappiness, along with her disinclination to accept the way things have gone, by claiming that things are not fair.

Etymologically, this general use of the concepts of fairness and unfairness is understandable enough. The notion of fairness is frequently used to indicate the absence of a blemish (e.g., "fair skin," "fair weather," or "fair skies") or to assert that things are proper, appropriate, or as they should be, or that things have gone according to hoyle (e.g., "fair ball," "fair enough," or "fair and square") (Hinton, 1990: p. 284). As some of these locutions indicate, a condition of fairness, understood in this general sense, is often a positive or desirable one. Fair skin, for example, is typically regarded as a feature of beauty, and most of us value fair weather in much the way sailors value fair winds. Sometimes, however, merely indicating the absence of a blemish also implies a moderate dissatisfaction with the way things are. Someone who only "feels fair," for example, has room for improvement even though she has nothing specific to complain about. And someone who receives only a "fair grade" on an exam could have done better.

This general, and perhaps most basic sense of fairness can be juxtaposed to something we might call "foulness" for lack of a more suitable term. As the contrary of fairness, foulness intimates that something is not as it should be ideally, that it is marred or scarred in some way, or that something has gone wrong. I do not mean to imply, however, that foulness and fairness are exact contraries; for this is certainly not true. We do not always think things are foul if they are blemished, and hence not fair. A person who does not have fair skin, for example, is not usually said to have foul skin. And while we can speak of foul odors, we do not ordinarily consider the absence of such foulness to mean that an odor is fair.

As a general assertion of disapprobation, a claim of unfairness obscures the difference between unfairness--the judgment that something is inconsistent with the demands of fairness--and foulness--the judgment that something is not fair because tarnished or blemished in some way. I take such general assertions of disapprobation, then, to involve claims of generic unhappiness where the fact that things did not go as one had wanted, or perhaps expected, indicate the presence of some blemish to which one objects. Thus it makes some sense for a student who has received a failing grade on a paper, in spite of his considerable effort to do well, to assert that the grade he received is unfair. (He is right, in any event, to note with understandable dismay that the grade is a foul one in the sense of being rotten, poor, or below par.) But he cannot mean by this that the grade is wrong, mistaken, or inappropriate if it is an accurate evaluation of the merits of his work, or more simply, if the grade is just.

While such protestations of unfairness frequently register little more than a person's unhappiness or dissatisfaction with a certain course of events, sometimes they have an independent merit. The claim that something is unfair, for example, displays a justifiable disappointment if it is inspired by some actual deficiency (or blemish) that could be given a more exact description. (Imagine someone complaining because the opera ticket promised her was given to someone else instead.) Here the presence of some more specific moral wrong is protested by indicating that the wrong in question constitutes a blemish that is properly objectionable. So, generic protestations of fairness or unfairness can be inspired by legitimate moral wrongs or by simple dissatisfaction about some particular course of events.

Understanding fairness in terms of the absence of a blemish introduces the most basic formal element associated with this notion. But it does not comprehend all the work we do with the word "fairness," and thus there is reason to think that there is another concept of fairness that has a different and independent formal element. (This more explicit notion of fairness will operate as a material element of the more generic concept of fairness when it constitutes the blemish generically identified, but we rarely view it in these terms.)

Sometimes claims like "that's unfair," like the corresponding claim "that's unjust," lodge specific complaints that carry with them some sense of the type of blemish or wrong supposedly present. Correspondingly, claims that something is fair sometimes imply not simply that things are as they should be, but more particularly that certain transgressions, violations, or disruptions are not present. When this more specific concept of fairness is at issue, deviations from the standards of fairness are properly considered unfair, and not simply foul.

The notion of fair play, for example, is ambiguous with regard to the generic notion of fairness just discussed and the more specific one to which I now want to call attention. Sometimes it refers to proper or appropriate play (fairness in the general sense), and sometimes it indicates a certain commitment to the spirit of competition, a concern not to cheat, and so forth. In the first instance, fair play can be juxtaposed with something like "foul play," where deviations from the standards of fair play constitute a foul or breach of the rules. (The notion of committing a foul present in the sport of basketball is illustrative in this regard.) But foul play is often different from unfair play. In the second instance, fair play implies that one is not cheating, deliberately manipulating the rules to one's advantage, or otherwise stretching the limits of propriety by seeking a competitive advantage inappropriate to the nature of the activity in which one is participating.

To illustrate the conceptual difference here, consider a basketball player who fouls an opponent while trying to block a shot. The shot block attempt was not fair; it involved a violation of the rules of play. When such a violation takes place, there is a sense in which the violator has not played fairly; his play is blemished by the breach of the rule. But we can suppose that the player was not also playing unfairly. That is, we can suppose that the player was trying to stay within the confines of the rules, not to foul, and to make a good (i.e., fair) play. Although the player committed a foul, although his play was not fair in this sense, he was still playing fairly.[3] Things are different, however, if a player deliberately and consistently fouls his opponent believing that the officials will not call all infractions of the rules and hoping thereby to gain an advantage over his opponent.

By intentionally fouling one's opponent in the hope of getting away with some fouls, by refusing to honor the rules in order to gain an advantage and enhance one's chances of winning, a competitor plays unfairly. This is a particular material element of unfairness that might be conceptualized in terms of taking advantage of the circumstances of play. This more specific notion of fairness and unfairness, involved in such material notions as fair play, bargaining or trading fairly, or simply *being* fair, seems to be the one with the greatest moral and political significance. That is, this seems to be the concept of fairness we need to understand if we are to gain a deeper understanding of the way fairness concerns factor into our moral and political lives. Accordingly, this is the concept of fairness that will concern me in what follows.

Nevertheless, these two senses of fairness are sure to be the source of some confusion as things progress. Since I am chiefly concerned with the more specific, moral notion of fairness, there is little reason to distinguish sharply between them. At times, however, it may not be clear from the text which concept of fairness I am using. To mitigate the likely confusion--unhappily I am not certain this confusion can be completely eliminated--I will specify when I am using the generic concept of fairness. In the absence of any such specification, readers can presume that I am discussing the specific, moral sense of fairness.

Fairness and Respect for Persons

One final preliminary remark is in order. Sometimes a concern for fairness seems to involve something like giving credit where credit is due or showing due care and concern for others. For example, we sometimes qualify our statements about others by saying, "in fairness to X," or "to be fair to X," and these qualifications suggest that fairness is something owed to specific others. If we recur to the concept of generic fairness, we can make some sense of these locutions; they state a concern about treating X properly or appropriately, whatever this might involve. But of course this gives no indication of what it is that is owed to others or why it is owed to them.

But sometimes when we talk about being fair to others we seem to have something more in mind than merely treating them properly under the circumstances. Sometimes the treatment owed them seems to be owed in a strong sense. It is not simply inappropriate to fail to accord them their due; it is positively wrong, and hence unfair. From a moral point of view, it often looks like this sense of fairness has particular currency. We might say, for example, that we ought to take seriously and respect the interests of others, and we might then think of this as a requirement of fairness if we suppose that fairness involves treating others with proper concern and respect. Here fairness does not merely indicate the absence of a particular type of moral blemish (say, the duty to treat others with respect), it positively identifies some moral duty as a requirement of fairness (Cf. Sullivan, 1975). This view of fairness is aptly illustrated by the sixth and final formal account of fairness listed above.

Because philosophers and others do use the concept of fairness in this way, there is no disputing its pertinence. And given the current interest in variations of Kantian moral thought, it is perhaps not surprising that moral philosophers working within this tradition would want to employ the concept of fairness in some such fashion. This by itself is hardly reason to conclude, of course, that this account of fairness makes much sense. But it is reason to treat this particular view of fairness as a distinct concept and to distinguish it from the other two concepts of fairness already introduced. So, when I want to speak of fairness in this deontic sense, I will refer to "Kantian fairness." This too is sure to be a source of confusion, but I can think of no less confusing way to keep these separate notions of fairness distinct.

Employed chiefly as a technical term within deontological moral theories, the concept of Kantian fairness does frequent duty in philosophical discourse. And there are those who suppose that thinking of fairness in terms of the respect owed to others gets to the heart of its formal element. I will have occasion to raise a number of objections to this view, and while this obviously does not mean that philosophers are not at liberty to use the concept of Kantian fairness in their theorizing, it should raise questions about whether such theories accurately describe the nature of our moral associations insofar as they involve fairness concerns. For the moment, however, it is enough to regard the concept of Kantian fairness as one of several possible accounts of the formal element of fairness, and one that will need to be considered when the time comes. Since there is no reason to presume, at the outset, that the notion of treating others with respect actually does get to the formal element of fairness, it seems appropriate to hold whatever deontological sympathies we might have in abeyance and let our analysis take us where it will.

Notes

1. There are, for example, various ways to lie to someone--overt lies, lies of omission, and so forth. So lying has a formal element. But it is also a type of deceit, and so it is also a material element of this larger notion. (One can deceive, of course, in ways that do not involve lying.) But deceit is also a type of moral wrong; so it is also a material element of this larger formal moral notion.

2. Wittgenstein insisted that "Philosophy may in no way interfere with the actual use of language; it can in the end only describe it" (1953: p. 49). It may be more to the point to say that philosophy can only attempt to describe the actual use of language, but insofar as we reflect on what we say and do, such description may enter the everyday world of language use and have an impact on what we do say.

3. Sometimes we say of those who have suffered from an accident, from an unusual natural disaster, and the like that their plight is unfair. We mean by this that their suffering is wrong, unfortunate, objectionable, and so forth, but not that they have been treated or been dealt with in some specifically wrong or objectionable fashion. These are, then, clearly generic uses of the notion of unfairness.

Chapter Two

Objectivity, Impartiality, and Fairness

People often claim to have been dealt with unfairly when they have been taken advantage of by others. Sometimes these claims are understood to assert that the person disadvantaged has been wronged in a specific way, viz., the person in question has been treated or dealt with unfairly. When this is the case, such claims are not merely general assertions of disapprobation, or general objections to the way things have gone. They imply that to be taken advantage of, at least in such instances, is to be done a particular type of wrong, a wrong understood in terms of unfairness. We might say, then, that fairness involves not taking advantage of others when it is possible or perhaps even desirable to do so.

This view of the matter seems intuitively attractive, but it does not provide much insight into the formal element of fairness. Specific instances of advantage taking may appear to be unfair, but they are not necessarily unfair *because* someone has taken advantage of another. There may also be material instances of unfairness that do not involve taking advantage of others. It is a mistake, then, to move too quickly from the observation that certain instances of advantage taking involve an unfairness to the conclusion that unfairness involves taking advantage of others. Nevertheless, the intuitive link between advantage taking and judgments about fairness suggests that this might be a profitable place to begin to consider the formal element of fairness.

Taking Advantage and Disadvantaging

There is a distinction of some importance between taking advantage of others and disadvantaging them. Gauthier understands the idea of taking advantage of others to involve "bettering one's situation through interaction that worsens the situation of another" (1986: p. 205). But this seems wrong. Not all interactions that benefit someone at the expense of another involve a situation where it is reasonable to say that the advantaged person has taken advantage of the person whose condition has been worsened. Suppose A and B are evenly matched in the one hundred meter dash and both are aware of this. Suppose further that A challenges B to a race and insists on betting B that he will win. There is no advantage taking in evidence if B accepts the challenge, matches the bet, and manages to win the race, but B is better off than he was before the race while A is clearly worse off (Cf. Sher, 1987: p. 36).

We would do better to think of advantage taking as a form of exploitation where the exploitation in question targets some attribute, aspect, or characteristic of the person being exploited. Taking advantage of a person generally involves identifying something about this person that is vulnerable and hence exploitable.[1] If a tennis player discovers that her opponent has a weak backhand, she will likely adjust her game in order to take advantage of this weakness.[2] This is hardly unfair, of course, or even wrong; it is simply good play. We would think it quite strange if A could exploit B's weak backhand and increase her chances of winning the match but failed to do so because she thinks it wrong to take advantage of someone in this manner.

Disadvantaging, on the other hand, seems a more general notion that does not necessarily involve any exploitation. Instead, to disadvantage others is to impede them in some way or to make things more difficult for them in their efforts to realize their ends. Taking advantage, then, can be a species of disadvantaging; by taking advantage of B's weak backhand, A puts B at a disadvantage in their match. But disadvantaging does not necessarily mean that the party that realizes a comparative gain from disadvantaging is doing the disadvantaging, or even that others gain as a consequence of the disadvantaging (comparative advantaging). An umpire, for example, might call a baseball game in a way that deliberately disadvantages one team, perhaps because he dislikes the team's manager. Here the umpire does not benefit in any obvious way from his actions--he may not even prevent the disadvantaged team from winning--while the team that does realize a comparative advantage has done nothing wrong--and may even be unaware of the advantage they receive. Similarly, an umpire might disadvantage both teams by, say, changing the way he interprets the strike zone each inning. Since neither team can now be certain about what counts as a strike, the job of hitting is made harder for both sides. Consequently, they are both disadvantaged in terms of their ability to get hits and score runs.

As should be evident, not all forms of disadvantaging, including some of those that qualify as advantage taking, are unfair (or even generically unfair); some disadvantaging, including some advantage taking, is entirely fair. Exploiting an opponent's weak backhand is an obvious example. But other instances of disadvantaging clearly are unfair, including some that involve no comparative advantaging. Fairness concerns often arise in what I will call contested situations or in contexts where comparative gain (or the avoidance of comparative loss) is sought at the presumed expense of others. For example, fairness is of central importance in competitive situations like games and bargaining, and is also pertinent in more general contested contexts like the distribution of scarce or indivisible goods, the awarding of prizes, granting of offices, allocation of honors, judging of comparative merit, and so forth. While we have no reason at this point to think that fairness concerns arise only in such contested contexts, they nevertheless figure prominently in our evaluations of how things have gone in these contexts.

Contested contexts invariably involve comparative advantaging and disadvantaging; that is, they involve making discriminations that may benefit some and that risk either worsening the situation of others or leaving their situation unchanged.

Fairness cautions us that there is a right way and a wrong way to participate in or proceed with certain contentious activities. In competitive games, for example, disadvantaging, and more specifically advantage taking, are inescapable features of play. But it is not disadvantaging one's opponent that is a cause for moral concern; rather, it is *unfairly* disadvantaging one's opponent that is objectionable. If B loses her tennis match to A, she can explain the loss by saying that A managed to exploit her backhand and she was unable to offset the advantage this afforded A. But this cannot be understood as a complaint, or as a claim that A won because she played unfairly. Instead, it must be understood as something of a compliment to A who succeeded in exploiting B's weak backhand and winning the match.

So it seems that we can begin to get clear on the nature of fairness and unfairness by thinking about why some instances of disadvantaging are fair and some are unfair. Perhaps the key difference here is that unfairness involves non-consensual disadvantaging while consensual disadvantaging is simply a form of "fair play." We could say, for example, that B cannot complain if A manages to exploit her backhand and gain a winning advantage because by choosing to play the match, B consents to the possibility of being disadvantaged in this manner. But B does not similarly consent to being cheated by A simply by entering the match, and because cheating is a form of non-consensual disadvantaging, it is unfair.

This argument, however, lacks the proper symmetry required to distinguish between fair and unfair disadvantaging. Consenting to the possibility of X happening and consenting to X's happening are two different things. It seems right to think that by entering her match with A, B accepts the possibility that her backhand will be exploited during play. But she does not similarly consent to having her backhand exploited; in fact, we can suppose that she will do everything in her power to prevent this. Her success in this regard is constrained by her own abilities (e.g., "running around" her backhand) and by the rules of play (e.g., she cannot *fairly* call shots to her backhand out or illegal).

Suppose now that B knows A has a perhaps deserved reputation for cheating (perhaps by "hooking" or calling shots that hit in the court out of court) and enters play anyway. By doing so, it seems she also consents to the possibility of being cheated. That is, this now seems to be a risk she is willing to run even though we can suppose she will do what she can to prevent A from cheating. (Perhaps B will say something to A about her line calls or tell her that she is ready to ask for a linesperson.) While it is clear that B does not consent to being cheated, if she does not want to consent to this possibility she had best not enter play.[3] Participants in a competitive game can invariably suppose that an opponent might resort to cheating, just as they can suppose that an opponent will look for more acceptable ways of winning. So, by entering play, it seems a competitor consents to the possibility of having a weakness exploited and to the possibility of being cheated, even though she does not also consent to having a weakness exploited or to being cheated.

Cheating, however, is generally understood to be unfair; it is a form of impermissible disadvantaging. It might even involve a type of advantage taking if, for example, A knows that B is rather timid and reluctant to challenge her opponent for cheating. If A takes advantage of this reluctance and cheats openly because she is confident that she can get away with it, she is disadvantaging her opponent and exploiting a "weakness" of character at the same time. But it no longer seems we can explain this by insisting that cheating is a form of non-consensual disadvantaging. This is because exploiting an opponent's backhand also seems to be a form of non-consensual disadvantaging but it also qualifies as fair play. Similarly, if we can say that exploiting one's backhand is fair because one consents to this possibility by joining the match, i.e., because this is an understood risk of play, then we must say the same thing with regard to cheating, for this too is a risk one runs by joining play. Once we get the symmetry right, it becomes evident that the issue of consent adds nothing to the equation that permits us to get clearer on the nature of fairness.

Our initial recourse to consent, however, may be better understood in terms of the reasonable expectations of the participants. By entering play, participants understand that things will proceed in a certain way, or at least that they should proceed in this way. And by entering play, participants consent to have things go as they should. Because the rules of play allow (even encourage) A to exploit B's weak backhand, B cannot complain that she did not leave herself open for this possibility by entering play. But cheating is *ultra vires*; it involves a deliberate defection from the way the competition is supposed to go. And perhaps there is something here that explains why cheating is unfair. We shall have occasion to explore this possibility in greater detail in future chapters. For present purposes, however, we should note that this account of unfairness moves us away from a focus on disadvantaging. If this view is sound, it is the defection, and not the disadvantaging, that constitutes the unfairness. And too, it moves us away from questions of consent. Presumably, a defection from the way things should go is unfair regardless of the consent of the participants.

Impartiality and Bias

We might also attempt to explain why some instances of disadvantaging are fair while others are not by arguing that unfair disadvantaging involves a breach of the objectivity crucial to our sense of fairness. Suppose, then, we propose an account of the formal element of fairness in terms of impartiality or objectivity. I will understand impartiality, following Nagel, to involve acting upon impartial or neutral reasons, and I will assume that such reasons can be discerned by appeal to standards of universality and objectivity. On the former condition, a reason is impartial if the agent contemplating acting upon it is willing to allow everyone to act upon it. On the latter condition, and again following Nagel, a reason is impartial if it is also a reason that anyone could have and act upon (Nagel, 1970: pp. 90-95; 1986: pp. 152-53; 1991:

pp. 10-11 and pp. 85-86; Cf. Darwall, 1983: pp. 210-211). Impartial reasons are blind to personal preferences, and thus they are to be distinguished from self-regarding reasons. Persons who act upon self-regarding reasons put themselves first and often privilege their own personal interests over the interests of others.

While disadvantaging is concerned entirely with affecting outcomes, impartiality is concerned chiefly with the reasons one has for doing something and not specifically with outcomes. If we think of fairness and unfairness in terms of impartiality and neutrality, then, we must associate it not with the desired results of one's actions but with the nature of the reasons one acts upon. Recourse to impartiality also broadens the range of possible fairness concerns beyond the limitations associated with instances of disadvantaging. If we believe that B's sense of her own well-being is not psychologically tied to a comparison with her sense of A's well-being, then a claim of unfairness can be made by B if C advantages A for partial reasons but does not similarly advantage B even though A and B are similarly situated. The advantaging of A here might seem unfair, because it results from C's partiality, even though B has not been made worse off.

Imagine, for example, that Amy and Bonnie take an objective test and both answer all the questions the same way. (They were not cheating, we can suppose; they just happen to think that the same answers are the correct ones.) Let us say that they answer seventy-five percent of the questions correctly, and Carla, their teacher, gives Amy a B for her work and Bonnie a B+. Since Bonnie has received the higher grade, she has been advantaged in comparison to Amy. But this doesn't mean that Amy has been disadvantaged by Carla. There does not seem to be any disadvantage on display, for example, if Amy and Bonnie are not competitors for some prize to be determined by the awarding of the grade. Even if they are competitors, say for admission to the same law school, Amy may have such a considerable lead over Bonnie that the slight advantaging Carla provides Bonnie will make little difference. And if the two are not competitors, the grade of B may be all that Amy needs to reach the goals she has set herself.

Sometimes, of course, a comparative advantaging will result in a disadvantaging. (Suppose, Amy and Bonnie both want to be admitted to the same law school and their credentials are equal accept for the grade received from Carla.) This is unfair, however, only if the disadvantage incurred is the result of an undeserved or improper comparative advantaging. (An appropriate or justifiable comparative advantaging never seems to be unfair.) But as the example indicates, there also seem to be situations of comparative advantaging that seem unfair even though no disadvantaging is involved. Intuitively, there is reason to suppose that Carla has been unfair in the way she has assigned grades to Amy and Bonnie. (Although I think this is right in general, we will have occasion to qualify this claim as the argument progresses.) Since the unfairness cannot be a consequence of the occurrent fact of disadvantaging, we might think it results from the presumption that Carla has not been impartial in assigning grades, that she has favored Bonnie for reasons that fail the test of objectivity.

So perhaps there is something to be said for thinking of fairness in terms of impartiality. But there are problems here as well. For one thing, it is rather natural, and hardly objectionable, to be partial to one's own position in many of those contested contexts where fairness concerns frequently arise. Competitors who want to win the event in which they compete are presumably biased in their own favor and they conduct themselves accordingly by playing to win. It is bias, after all, that explains why A wants to exploit B's weak backhand. But one can be biased in one's own favor and still play fairly. Moreover, being biased and being fairminded do not seem to be mutually exclusive mental states. A competitor can play to win by advantaging himself as best he can and still be committed to a fair competition. Here the competitor's dedication to fairness commits him to fairly advantaging himself only. Of course, a competitor may even have partial or biased reasons for playing fairly, as is the case if a player believes she will feel better when (and if) she wins if she plays fairly and does not cheat. Here bias and fairmindedness seem to be at odds, but even people who are not terribly fairminded can play, compete, bargain, or deal fairly.

There are also situations where partial or biased conduct seems morally acceptable--perhaps even morally required--and so hardly unfair. Consider, for example, Nagel's notion of "agent relative" considerations that involve legitimate, perhaps (it seems) even morally necessary, bias in favor of ourselves or those close to us (1986: pp. 158-59; 1991: pp. 85-86; Cf. Williams, 1981: pp. 1-19; Friedman, 1991: pp. 818-35). Suppose L notices that a boat carrying his mother and a complete stranger has overturned casting both passengers into the water. Suppose further that neither can swim and that L can manage to save only one of the two. He has agent relative reasons for saving his mother, and this is probably what we would expect from him. We might even think it morally wrong if he flipped a coin to see which passenger he would save; his reasons for saving his mother are compelling even though they are biased.

Here it does not seem that L's biased decision to save his mother raises any concern about the fairness of his actions. For reasons we need to understand, I do not think that we would say here that L acted unfairly but understandably under the circumstances. That is, L's special (and partial) relation to his mother does not permit the justifiable overriding of the demands of fairness. Instead, fairness does not seem to be an issue here; the moral claims it makes upon us simply do not operate under these circumstances.

The example can be made somewhat messier, however, if we suppose that L is a doctor responsible for making allocations of scarce drugs and that he must decide which of two patients will receive the last dose of a drug that both need in order to live. We can again suppose that one patient is L's mother while the other is a stranger. This, of course, is clearly a contested context but things are now complicated because both L's mother and the stranger have a claim upon the drug that he must recognize in his capacity as the doctor responsible for distributing drugs. So the question now becomes whether his responsibilities as a doctor trump L's status as a son of one of the needy parties when it comes to considering what he ought to do.

Yet even under these circumstances, it does not seem that recourse to impartiality is terribly helpful in terms of thinking about what fairness requires here. For what we want to know is whether L should make his decision impartially or whether it is still permissible for him to give the drug to his mother because it is his mother, i.e., to give the drug to her for biased reasons. We simply beg this question if we insist that, under the circumstances, fairness requires that L act impartially. We would think it unfair of L to give the last dose of the drug to his mother for reasons of partiality only if we decide independently that his role as doctor requires him to regard his personal relation to his mother as irrelevant to the distribution process. Although the point may seem wrong at present, I want to argue that a fairness concern arises in situations like this only once some such moral judgment has been made. The concerns of fairness, then, do not supply the moral insights that permit us to make such judgments.

But this point might seem to move fairness closer to impartiality. I am suggesting that L's role as doctor may introduce moral concerns that require him to be impartial in the distribution of the needed drug. Let us suppose that this is so. We can now say that while fairness does not require him to be impartial, under the circumstances, he acts unfairly if he does not distribute the drug impartially. And partiality now looks like the particular moral blemish we would identify if we say L distributed the drug unfairly by giving it summarily to his mother. But it is too much of a leap to conclude from this that impartiality constitutes the formal element of fairness. The need to be impartial, as required by those moral concerns that exclude familial relations as pertinent to the distribution of the drug, dictate that the distribution of the drug should be made fairly, i.e., in a manner faithful to the moral concerns that advise impartiality. But we cannot derive the conclusion that fairness should be formally understood in terms of impartiality from the fact that impartiality requires L to act fairly under the circumstances.

There is one final problem with attempts to explain fairness in terms of impartiality or objectivity that needs to be considered. It seems possible to identify some instances of unfairness that do not exhibit any partiality, bias, or prejudice. The example of the baseball umpire who changes his interpretation of the strike zone each inning offers a salient case in point. The altered strike zone is imposed on each team when it comes to bat, and we can suppose that the umpire is not engaging in this foolishness in order to enhance the chances of either team's winning the game. That is, the umpire might be completely objective in the sense that his actions are not intended to favor one team over the other. Nor is it possible to discern a clear disadvantaging from the umpire's actions. Both teams would appear to suffer similarly.[4] Yet the umpire's behavior still seems unfair even if we are not able to find any bias in the reasons he has for altering the strike zone. If this is right, and if the umpire's actions are unfair (if, that is, they constitute a specific type of wrong that both teams and others associated with the game suffer) and not merely foul (a blemish on the game), then there is something to fairness that cannot be explained by thinking of fairness merely in terms of impartiality and objectivity.

I think this is right; that is, I think the umpire is being unfair, although at this point in the discussion I am willing to admit that the point may seem far from certain. I suspect, however, that anyone playing or watching the game and noticing what the umpire was doing would almost surely object to his behavior. And it seems altogether appropriate to press the objection in terms of fairness. If so, it is the umpire's actions that are unfair, and they are unfair independent of his reasons for acting. Sometimes a person will act unfairly by acting on reasons that incline him to put himself first. This is frequently the case in contested contexts where participants have personal reasons to defect from the process at hand or take liberties with the rules of play. But it is possible to act unfairly, it seems, by acting upon reasons that do not involve or exhibit any bias or partiality.[5] A competitor may have external reasons for winning a competition; perhaps, for example, she can prevent a great evil from happening if she wins. She might then have good reason to cheat, and we might even believe this is the right thing for her to do. But we would still think her cheating unfair. Only here, she has compelling moral reason to set aside the demands of fairness and to play unfairly. There is no real partiality here, though there is a disadvantaging, but there is still an unfairness. So it seems fairness is concerned chiefly with what we do, and only secondarily, if at all, with our reasons for doing it.

Disadvantaging and Personal Interests

Sometimes claims about being unfairly disadvantaged appear to be based on the idea that one's interests have not been properly respected. Taking this as a clue, we could say that fairness involves respecting, or taking seriously, the interests of others. Perhaps this is just another way to tie fairness to impartiality; nevertheless, it is not an altogether implausible suggestion. Since fairness concerns often arise in contested contexts where personal interests might incline individuals to favor themselves or particular others, we should entertain the possibility that fairness counsels us to weight the interests of all relevant individuals, oneself included, equally or identically, even though we might not want to do so.

Some qualifications are in order, however, if we are to avoid the problems already encountered. As we have seen, it is understood, in contested contexts, that the parties involved have interests in conflict. Consequently, not all participants can realize their desires. Nor do we expect, under these circumstances, that participants will remain strictly impartial; they want, we can suppose, to win, and they will play or participate accordingly. But the rules of play establish the proper parameters of tolerable impartiality. Put somewhat differently, the rules determine what one may do, and what one may not do, to further one's interest in coming out on top. The rules of tennis, for example, allow a competitor to exploit an opponent's weak strokes, but they do not correspondingly allow a competitor to call out shots that the rules define as good. The pursuit of one's interests in accordance with the rules, then, would seem to demonstrate a suitable respect for the interests of one's opponent. Only the standards of play, and not irrelevant considerations, will determine whose ends will be realized, and this seems to correspond with out intuitions about fair play.

While all of this seems plausible enough, there is also a subtle complexity on display here. It is possible, in fact, to find three separate accounts of the formal element of fairness lurking behind these remarks. They are, in no particular order:

1. Fairness involves equal respect for the interests of all parties when these interests are in conflict.
2. Fairness involve adherence to rule.
3. Fairness involves fidelity to social practice.

I will have more to say about (2) and (3) as the discussion progresses; at present, I want to focus exclusively on (1).

To begin, (1) may be reducible to more basic normative concerns. For example, the idea of equality might explain the force we ascribe to it. Thus, (1) could simply express a material element of fairness that is comprehended by the formal notion of fairness as equality. Similarly, the idea of respect for persons itself might carry the normative weight here and constitute the formal element of fairness (i.e., Kantian fairness) that gives meaning to (1). Finally, (1) may not be reducible at all. The normative clout associated with (1) may simply follow from the fact that fairness requires us to consider the interests of others as equal to ours when they come into conflict. This may be regarded simply as a requirement of logic; from an external point of view, the interests of all individuals stand equal.

Let me dwell on the third possibility for the moment and leave the other two for later. Consider the following situation. Imagine that student Y asks instructor X for a letter of recommendation to a particular graduate school. Let us suppose that this is the only school Y wants to attend and that he desperately wants to attend this school. Let us also suppose that X knows that if she writes a suitably strong letter, Y will be admitted to his chosen school. Finally, I also want to suppose that X knows that other instructors invariably exaggerate their students' abilities in such letters, perhaps hoping to facilitate their students' admission or perhaps simply not wanting to err in a direction that hinders their students' ability to gain their desired admission. If X writes what she considers to be an accurate letter, it will not be strong enough to assure Y's admission. Moreover, an accurate letter seemingly disadvantages Y. Given the fact of evaluation inflation, equally talented students will receive stronger letters while less talented students may receive equally strong letters or even stronger ones. If X inflates Y's abilities in roughly the way the letters from other instructors inflate their students' abilities, we can assume he will gain admission (X's letter will be suitably strong). Moreover, by inflating her evaluation, X will not have hindered the interests other students have in gaining admission to the school in question. An inflated letter simply evens things out; because no one's abilities are comparatively favored, no one's interests are comparatively advantaged or disadvantaged by X's actions.

If we focus exclusively on comparative interests, (1) would instruct X to write a letter inflating Y's abilities in order to be fair. This is the only move where everyone's interests are equally respected by X. But from a different viewpoint, this not only seems wrong, it seems positively unfair. We sometimes evaluate someone's evaluative judgments of another as fair or unfair in their own right and absent any concern for comparative disadvantaging. We would most likely consider a letter of recommendation a "fair letter" if it describes accurately and faithfully a student's abilities, accomplishments, and scholarly or professional potential. Perhaps we mean here only that such letters are generically fair, but I think we mean more than this. To fail to write an accurate letter is to be unfair and not just to do something generically wrong. That is, we expect such letters to be accurate, and if they are not, we think there is something unfair going on. If this is right, then X acts unfairly if she inflates Y's letter. So, there is reason to wonder what fairness requires of X in this situation. If our intuitions incline us to link fairness with (1), the inflated letter would be in order, and I want to see if this is so.

One way to oppose the case for an inflated letter involves an appeal to desert. The letter Y deserves is determined by his abilities, accomplishments, and potential for success in graduate school; that is, the merit associated with these criteria serves as what Feinberg calls a "desert basis" that should control the nature of the letter (Feinberg, 1970: pp. 57-61). Desert considerations typically introduce, as we shall see, concerns of justice. If Y gets the letter he deserves, he cannot claim to have been done an injustice, and because he got what he deserves, there is no additional room for complaint.

However, Y might not see things this way, and if we accept (1), the notion of fairness would be on his side. While Y could not claim he had been dealt with unjustly, he could still insist that he has been treated unfairly since he has been disadvantaged by X's letter. Since (1) still seems intuitively plausible, we must suppose that Y's concerns are credible and that fairness concerns carry weight in this situation independent of justice concerns. This possibility raises some important questions about the relation of justice to fairness. But these questions matter only if we subscribe to (1), and the jury is still out.

Perhaps we can remove the appearance of a conundrum in this situation by holding that some interests are still disadvantaged under the scenario where all students receive similarly inflated letters. We might contend, for example, that the interests of the members of admissions committees are compromised by exaggerated letters. Therefore, the requirements of (1) are not met by the inflated letter. This possibility has merit if admissions officers have a stake in the recommendation process and are disadvantaged by the submission of inflated letters. It seems reasonable to suppose that admissions officers do have such an interest. They presumably want to see the admissions process go well and to have the opportunity to attract and admit capable applicants. We might understand this in two possible ways. First, admissions officers might want to see an egalitarian condition observed. Under this condition, candidate ranking is all that matters. Since equally inflated letters would still permit an accurate ranking of candidates, admission officers would not be disadvantaged under these circumstances, and the requirements of (1) would be met if X wrote an inflated letter. So this does not remove our apparent conundrum.

But admission officers might prefer accuracy to egalitarianism. The purpose of such letters, we might suppose, is to enable future mentors to get an accurate picture of an applicant's abilities, accomplishments, and potential. If admission officers are also future mentors, they might care about this. And even if they are not, they may still want to be sure that future mentors will be able to work with and help future students. They can be sure of this only if they have an accurate sense of student talents, abilities, and potential. If we adopt this view, then (1) permits us to conclude that fairness would require X to write an accurate letter. But this still does not save (1). If X writes an accurate letter, and if other instructors still inflate their letters, Y is still comparatively disadvantaged, and this is unfair under (1).

It is worth noting that things go better under both (2)--adherence to rule, and (3)--fidelity to social practice. Both of these conditions would require X to write an accurate letter in spite of the comparative disadvantaging Y will suffer as a result; therefore, both would require us to conclude that fairness demands an accurate letter. (I assume here that the mass defections from the practice I have supposed are just that--mass defections--and not a transformation of the nature of the practice itself.) Of course, Y could, and perhaps would, still protest that this is unfair, but I think his claim must be taken to mean that this is generically unfair only. If accurate letters are required as a matter of fairness, the blemish Y senses in his situation is not a consequence of X's actions. By writing an accurate letter, X also writes a fair letter. The problem lies with the other instructors that have written unfair letters.

Other things being equal, Y's interests are irrelevant to X's responsibilities as a referee, and it seems strange to think they suddenly become relevant if other referees defect from the proper operation of the practice of requiring letters of recommendation. If everyone else playing the game cheats, there is little reason to continue with the game. But it makes a mockery of things to insist that a person who decides to "play" and to cheat also is playing fairly if her cheating evens things out in terms of her chances of winning.

Perhaps there is something here, however, that would incline us to resurrect (1). Suppose we say that the unfairness on display in this situation is caused by other referees who violate (1) by wrongly advantaging their students. But this does not get us terribly far. At some initial point, referees do not necessarily know whether an inflated letter comparatively advantages their students. This all depends on the nature of the letters written by others. If they all knew letters were being inflated to a certain degree, (1) would still require them to write inflated letters, and this takes us back to square one. This follows because (1) calls into play only *comparative* advantaging and disadvantaging.

We can avoid this problem only by introducing the notion of baseline advantaging and disadvantaging. Under this scenario, applicants are advantaged or disadvantaged depending upon the way an inflated letter deviates from the accuracy requirement that sets each candidate's proper baseline. But we cannot adopt this view and still save (1) because it is no longer the advantaging or disadvantaging that accounts for our fairness judgments under these circumstances. If X writes an accurate letter and all other referees inflate their students' letters, the situation is unfair, and Y can now lodge a more specific complaint. It is a mistake, however, to understand the unfairness here as a consequence of the disadvantaging Y suffers. Granted, Y pays the price, but the unfair advantaging others receive is a consequence of the other referees whose letters deviate from the baseline requirements of such letters. We can get to this by appeal to either (2) or (3), but not (1). That is, Y's complaint might be either that other referees failed to adhere to the rules that govern the writing of letters of recommendations or that the other referees defected from the social practice in which they were involved.

So much, then, for thinking of fairness in terms of an equal concern for the interests of all parties involved, at least in a contested context. We might still want to argue, however, that fairness is concerned with an equal respect for the interests of others because questions of fairness sometimes seem to arise outside of specific contested contexts. (Imagine two strangers trying to decide how to divide a cake both of them happen to want.) In such situations, (1) again seems intuitively attractive; so if we are to prefer (2) or (3) to (1) as formal accounts of fairness, we must say something more about this. We will have occasion, then, to return to this matter as the argument progresses.

Notes

1. For a discussion of the relation between exploitation and vulnerability, see Feinberg, 1988: pp. 199-205. See also, Wertheimer, 1996: pp. 16-18.

2. If the player manages to exploit this weakness with enough success to win the match, she has bettered her situation at the expense of her opponent. But it seems wrong to say that her opponent's situation is worsened, since it is basically the same as it was before the match. Winning in competition does typically benefit the victor, but since the vanquished had no prior right to the fruits of victory, we cannot also say that losing worsens one's position.

3. It may sound strange to think that one consents to the possibility of being cheated by entering play with a known cheater. But if B understands that this is a possibility if she consents to play, then this is one of the possibilities to which she consents by entering play. That is, this is a risk she knowingly and willingly chooses to run.

4. One team might be better able to adjust to the umpire's whimsy, but we can suppose that the umpire is unaware of this. But even if he knew of this, it doesn't follow that he is changing his interpretation of the strike zone each inning in order to favor this team.

5. The case for the unfairness of the umpire's actions may be strengthened by adding to the example the further fact that the umpire is deliberately changing his interpretation of the strike zone each inning, perhaps because he enjoys watching the players' resultant frustration. If it seems clearer here that the umpire is behaving unfairly, it is still true that he is not behaving partially.

Chapter Three

Fair Shares

We sometimes think it unfair when people do not receive what we take to be their "fair share" of some good they have helped to bring about. We also tend to think that people who do not do their "fair share" of the work, or assume their share of some burden, are sometimes being unfair. These are rather commonplace observations that introduce a particular material element of fairness. Put more generally, we can say that fairness requires, at least on some occasions, that people get their share of some good they helped produce and do their share of the work associated with the production of some shared good. In this chapter, I want to see if it is possible to make sense of this. More particularly, I want to see if we can understand why doing or receiving one's share sometimes invokes fairness concerns as well as when, or under what circumstances, it does so.

The Principle of Fairness

Some philosophers insist that there is a normative relation between benefits conferred from cooperative ventures and the responsibility of benefitted individuals to contribute to such ventures. Moreover, they associate their concerns with the demands of fairness, perhaps to characterize the normative clout, or the sense of obligatoriness, they believe to be involved in such situations. The linkage between benefit and obligatory contribution seems to have been initially imagined by C.D. Broad who suggested that fairness involves "the principle that the best possible state of affairs is reached when the group of producers and that of enjoyers is as nearly identical as possible" (1916: p. 388). While Broad supposed common sense to endorse some such view of fairness, he was also characteristically cautious about a principle that he thought "bristles with difficulties" (1916: p. 397). H.L.A. Hart, on the other hand, has been less cautious. He claims that, "when a number of persons conduct any joint enterprise according to rules and thus restrict their liberty, those who have submitted to these restrictions when required have a right to a similar submission from those who have benefitted by their submission" (1955: p. 185). Hart refers to the resultant principle as a "mutuality of restrictions." It precludes a particular type of free-riding; people who benefit from the fact that others submit to certain rules are presumed to stand under an obligation to submit to these rules themselves.

Yet there is something odd going on here. Hart's principle facially violates the familiar belief that the only justifiable restrictions upon individual freedom are those to which a person voluntarily consents. So a satisfactory defense of the principle will necessarily have to supply the normative justification for the belief that the voluntary actions of some can have consequences that place obligations upon others.

This problem has not kept Hart's principle from gaining a measure of popularity. Rawls, for example, has offered his own version of Hart's principle and recoupled it with the idea of fairness. According to Rawls, "The main idea," behind the principle of fairness, "is that when a number of persons engage in a mutually advantageous cooperative venture according to rules, and thus restrict their liberty in ways necessary to yield advantages for all, those who have submitted to these restrictions have a right to a similar acquiescence on the part of those who have benefitted from their submission" (1971: p. 112; see also Rawls, 1958: p. 179). So over the years Broad's common sense conviction about the nature of fairness seems to have hardened into a strong moral right.

Yet, Rawls's principle is not without its problems. Robert Nozick, one of Rawls's staunchest critics on this score, has advanced two key arguments against Rawls's principle of fairness. His first argument exploits an ambiguity in Rawls's (as well as Hart's) principle as formulated and presented. He notes that the principle is indifferent to the nature of the benefit received and the burden required (1974: p. 94). The principle apparently imposes an obligation upon someone even if she receives a very small benefit from the collective efforts of others and even if the cost of her compliance is great. In effect, the principle as stated pays no attention to a ratio that Nozick considers significant; there is no requirement that the burden assumed be weighted in comparison to the benefit gained. Because it seems wrong to suppose that the collective efforts of some can impose a burden upon a person that makes her worse off in spite of the benefit gained, it also seems that we could not possibly regard such a situation as fair.

We can, however, amend the principle to guarantee that the benefits gained to someone must outweigh the costs assumed. Richard Arneson, for one, has re-worked the principle in just this fashion:

> Where a scheme of cooperation is established that supplies a collective benefit that is worth its cost to each recipient, where the burdens of cooperation are fairly divided, where it is unfeasible to attract voluntary compliance to the scheme via supplementary private benefits, and where the collective benefit is either voluntarily accepted or such that voluntary acceptance of it is impossible, those who contribute their assigned fair share of the costs of the scheme have a right, against the remaining beneficiaries, that they should also pay their fair share (1982: p. 623).

While Arneson's principle seems to resolve the confusion Nozick has spotted in Rawls's principle of fairness, it rather unhappily introduces considerably more confusion of a different sort. In particular, Arneson leaves us wondering how we are to decide what constitutes a fair division of cooperation and a fair share of the cost of the scheme. If a common sense understanding of fairness is to be our guide here, we will become lost rather quickly.

One way to understand a fair share of the cost of a given scheme is to divide the total cost by the number of beneficiaries and assign all beneficiaries an equal share. But this is obviously off-target. Nozick's concerns now re-emerge; someone who benefits only slightly may actually lose in the end. Since Arneson is clear that the collective benefit gained must be worth its cost to each recipient, this will not do.

A more promising possibility is suggested by Broad who supposed that fairness requires something like a similar ratio of benefit to burden for each participant (1916: p. 388). If the ratio of benefit to burden is the same for all beneficiaries, the scheme would seem to qualify as fair, and this suggests that the formal element of fairness might profitably be understood in terms of equality. For any cooperative scheme where the benefits to respective cooperators are determinable, it is mathematically possible to affix burdens in a manner that at least closely approximates an equal ratio of benefit to burden for all beneficiaries. In practice, of course, this may prove difficult to accomplish, but I will suppose for the time being that this is not sufficient reason to reject the suggestion.

There is, in any event, a more pressing difficulty that needs to be considered. As the actual benefit a person may realize from a cooperative scheme decreases, the required ratio of benefit to burden may yield an actual benefit so modest that a potential beneficiary is indifferent about cooperation. Under these circumstances, a potential beneficiary may reasonably decide not to participate on the grounds that the modest pay-off isn't worth the effort. Yet the principle of fairness requires us to say that this is unfair, and there is reason to wonder if we really want to say this.

The following example will help to illustrate the nature of the problem I have in mind. Suppose five people stand to benefit from a collective project, four of whom will benefit by twenty units of manna and one of whom, namely S, will benefit by one unit. Suppose further that the cost to the four major beneficiaries is ten units of labor, while the cost to S is one-half a unit of labor. This guarantees the proper ratio of benefits to burdens. Let us also stipulate that the good involved is nonexcludable; while S can refuse to participate in the scheme, she cannot be denied the receipt of one unit of manna.[1] Now imagine that S does not consider her gain to be large enough to make her assumption of the burden worth the trouble; therefore, she opts not to participate in the scheme, knowing that if the others go forward, she will take a free ride for one unit of manna. Let's say the others decide to go forward with the scheme, thinking that it is still worth it even if they have to divide the surplus one-half unit of labor amongst themselves.

Is S being unfair if the others realize the project and she still refuses to supply the half unit of labor that is her share of the burden? If we suppose that receipt of one unit of (nonexcludable) manna at the cost of a half unit of labor makes the project worth her while in spite of her protestations to the contrary, then Arneson's principle of fairness would require S to assume the burden. But the others went into the project knowing full well that S did not plan to participate. They made the deliberate decision that it was worth their while to proceed even at the additional cost required to cover S's share of the burden. If the value of some project is worth the effort of those contemplating bringing it about, and they proceed accordingly, what justification can they possibly have for taxing anyone who happens to profit from their project (Cf. Elster, 1989: pp. 26-27)?

The principle of fairness, of course, presumably supplies the needed justification. But the acceptability of the principle, under the circumstances, seems in doubt. In S's case, her decision not to participate is understandable enough since the benefit she will receive only slightly outweighs her costs. It is easy to see that this might not make participation worth her while, even though it surely is (as I have supposed) in occurrent terms.

But it is the fact that S chooses not to participate, coupled with the fact that others voluntarily proceed with the scheme anyway because doing so is worth their while, that appears to get S off the hook here, and not the fact that we can see that her decision not to participate seems reasonable. For there is something to be said for the view that S should be free to pursue her own interests in her own way, and others should be free to do so as well. If several individuals pool their efforts in order to realize some collective good, and if they understand going in that the effort is worth their while even if a potential beneficiary prefers not to participate, their voluntary choice to proceed seems to co-opt any additional concerns about the fairness of the distribution of resulting benefits.

Needless to say, this view of the matter encourages free-riding. Suppose, for example, S would benefit from a given cooperative scheme, but she also realizes that others are committed to the scheme because of the considerable benefits they will realize even if she does not participate. Suppose too that she is willing to do without the benefit if others do not think the project is worth pursuing in the event she opts not to participate. It may now be in S's best interest not to cooperate and let others decide whether they will pursue the project independently. If they do not, S lives with the status quo, but if they do, S enjoys a greater benefit than she would realize if she participated since she no longer assumes a portion of the cost. The rational thing for S to do here is to take a free ride, provided, of course, she is willing to live with the status quo. This is also the sort of thing defenders of the principle of fairness hope to prevent by appealing to fairness. But given the voluntary and informed character of the actions of the cooperators (viz., knowing that S will not participate and still thinking the project worth their while in spite of the increased cost associated with picking up S's share of the burden), it is not at all evident that S's free ride qualifies as unfair.

As should be evident, things go no better if we think S's decision that the benefit is not worth her share of the burden is sufficient to satisfy Arneson's initial condition that "a collective benefit . . . is worth its cost to each recipient. . . " If the worth of the benefit is left to individual choice, Arneson's principle would exempt S from bearing a share of the cost of the scheme. Now the principle is consistent with the concerns introduced by considerations of voluntary choice. But this move effectively renders the principle of fairness pointless. The aim of the principle, after all, is to block free-riding. If S can exempt herself from a share of the burden by refusing to participate on the grounds that participation is not worth her while, and if others proceed with the scheme on the grounds that it is still worth it to them even if they have to pick up S's share of the burden, the principle of fairness would become pointless.

Fairness and Equality

This problem raises an important question about the "normative clout" of the principle of fairness. We need to understand why someone incurs an obligation to assume a portion of the cost of some cooperative project simply because she benefits from it and regardless of whether she consents to cooperate in the project. This brings me to Nozick's second objection to Rawls's argument. Nozick thinks it is unjustifiably coercive to force free-riding beneficiaries to pay a share of the cost of some collective good if they have not previously consented to cooperate in the scheme that brought about the benefit. It is, he thinks, quite unacceptable to "impose" a benefit upon someone and then extract payment without asking whether one wanted the benefit in the first place (1974: p. 93).

His argument reduces to the interesting claim that the fact of the benefit does not, by itself, create an obligation to assume a portion of its cost, even if the benefit involved is a collective good that cannot be withheld from non-cooperating beneficiaries. Kent Greenawalt is largely in agreement with Nozick on this point. Greenawalt restricts his understanding of the principle of fairness to situations involving the voluntary acceptance of wanted benefits, stating, "When someone really does not want a benefit, its unavoidable receipt cannot give rise to a duty of fair play to contribute one's share" (1987: p. 125).

On its face, Greenawalt's qualification is curious. What sense does it make to think a person might not want to be benefitted in some fashion? This becomes understandable if we suppose (as I did above) that someone does not want a benefit enough to assume her proper portion of the burden of producing it. In the case of excludable goods, cooperators can simply be certain that such people do not receive a share of the benefits resulting from their scheme (provided the cost of excluding non-cooperators does not make exclusion counter-productive). When it comes to nonexcludable goods, however, they cannot prevent "free-riding" if someone decides not to participate in the scheme because doing so is not (considered) worth her while. Although there is surely a sense in which such a person wants the benefit, its unavoidable receipt would still not trigger the conclusion that she is obligated, on grounds of fairness, to pay her share of the cost of bringing it about.

This position is of interest, once again, because it explicitly denies the very point that at least some supporters of the principle of fairness want to defend. The principle is normally presumed to express the normative conditions that justify the claim that someone who receives a benefit should contribute her or his share of the cost of bringing the benefit about, regardless of whether acceptance of the benefit is voluntary. Once again, we can suppose there is something about the notion of fairness that establishes the required normative force for the principle--hence the point behind considering it a principle of *fairness*. But what?

One possibility is suggested by George Klosko who says that, "the principle [of fairness] expresses a general idea of fairness: similar individuals should be treated similarly. It is wrong for certain people to be exempt from burdens others must bear in the absence of morally relevant differences between them" (1992: p. 34). Thus understood, the concept of fairness approximates the notion of formal justice and requires the equal treatment of equal cases and proportionately different treatment of proportionately different cases (Cf. Carr, 1981: pp. 211-24). So, anyone who benefits from the efforts of others should assume a portion of the burden commensurate with the ratio of benefit to burden realized by others.

But none of this sheds any light on the normative force underlying the principle of fairness; it merely presents the principle as a material element of a more formal principle requiring similar treatment for similar cases. Although this latter principle is usually presented in the form of an imperative ("Treat similar cases similarly . . ."), there is reason to wonder about the source of *its* normative force.

One way to explain the normative force behind the proportional equality of treatment is to hold that this is a requirement of logical consistency or rationality, as Aristotle supposed. We should treat equal cases equally (and different cases differently but in proportion to the nature of the difference) because consistency demands it. Perhaps, then, fairness is understandable as the virtue of "applied rationality;" it requires the proper balancing between similar parties and the burdens and benefits they receive.

However, while logical consistency may be a virtue in mathematics, it is hardly a virtue when it comes to moral matters. Equal treatment may also be horrible treatment, and it would be foolish to think that P should treat S terribly because he has already treated R terribly and S is relevantly similar to R (Frankena, 1962: pp. 9-13; Carr, 1981: p. 212). When we think about how we should treat others, it is not logical consistency that matters but moral propriety. If we have moral reasons for treating someone a particular way, these reasons will apply equally to all similar cases. But the reasons in question, and not the fact of logical consistency, supply the normative grounds that dictate what we ought to do. If we act wrongly or badly, if that is we treat others in morally improper ways, we have no reason to propagate the injury by inflicting similar wrongs on relevantly similar others. The equal treatment of equal cases, then, is a consequence of acting upon general moral reasons or following acceptable moral rules, and we get things backwards if we suppose that it is itself a moral reason for treating others in a particular way (Cf. Hart, 1961: p. 156; Perelman, 1963: p. 41; Rawls, 1971: p. 58; Gewirth, 1978: pp. 161-62).[2]

So, the notion of formal equality of treatment reduces to something like adherence to rule, or perhaps fidelity to social practice, and consistency is a consequence--not a condition--of morally proper conduct. Consequently, it cannot supply the normative force necessary to power the principle of fairness; nor, more importantly, can it shed much light on the formal element of fairness. This conclusion can be defeated, however, if it is possible to imagine or identify cases where an action sets a precedent in the absence of a rule that should be followed in similar situations in order to be fair. We have already considered this possibility in Chapter Two, but perhaps it is time to discuss it further.

Imagine a random case of altruism. Suppose Smith is approached by a panhandler who requests a handout. Without reflection, let us say, Smith reaches into his pocket, pulls out a five dollar bill and hands it to the panhandler. Suppose further that a second panhandler, equally as needy as the first, notices this and approaches Smith. But this time Smith informs the panhandler that he has nothing for him, even though he has (and he knows he has) another five dollar bill in his pocket. I doubt anyone would think Smith is being unfair here. Random acts of altruism, like supererogatory moral acts, don't establish a precedent that triggers fairness concerns when they are not repeated in similar situations. Displays of kindness are not governed by either the demands of consistency or the concerns of fairness (although the second panhandler may complain that the situation is generically unfair).

In this case, there is no rule, no participatory practice, that obligates Smith and results in consistent conduct when followed. Consider, however, a slightly different case, one that has been introduced previously. Suppose X and Y take a test in Z's class and write essentially the same exams. They don't cheat; they simply cover the same points with about the same degree of depth and precision. Suppose further that Z assigns a grade of B- to X's paper. Because the exams are relevantly similar, logical consistency would apparently require Z to give the same grade to Y; and her failure to do so might now seem unfair.

Yet this now looks like little more than a case of rule following. Even if Z had no sense of the grade X's exam deserved when she read it, her evaluation determines the rule that guides her treatment of X's exam as well as Y's. That is, the evaluation process fixes the merit the exam displays and indicates the proper reward. Grades are not randomly assigned; they indicate the instructor's sense of how well a student met the challenge of the assignment. The application of standards, then, serves as the rule that presumably explains (and justifies) the instructor's evaluations. But this requires some justification. Why should the standards Z uses to judge the worth of X's exam govern her evaluation of other exams? The necessary justification, it might be argued, calls logical consistency back into play. Consistency requires Z to apply the same standards to all exams and to fail to do so is to be unfair.

But the appeal to consistency at this point is inapposite. Students presumably have an interest in doing well on exams, or doing better than other students, that stands independent of the role exams are supposed to play in the education process. And teachers may also have independent reasons for giving students either good or bad scores on their exams (e.g., they have their favorites). The examination process, or the education process more generally, thus has something of a contested nature; participants have reason to cheat if they can get away with it. Given the (ideal) nature of the educational process, however, these reasons do not count; they should not control the process by which exams are evaluated and grades assigned. Discriminations are made and degrees of excellence are assigned (ideally) according to standards that are appropriate to the practice.

If a teacher changes her standards of evaluation in mid-stream, or if she deliberately judges some students inaccurately, she is not being faithful to the nature of the grading process. She is, in effect, not playing fair. Assuming that the point behind evaluating exams is to rank student achievement as measured by the exam, exams should be judged according to the same appropriate standard. This, however, is required by fidelity to the educational process, and not by logical consistency. Once again, consistency will be the consequence of fidelity to this particular social practice, but it plays no determinative role in guiding our thoughts on the fairness of an instructor's evaluation of student work.

Things would be different, on the other hand, if the purpose of the examination process was otherwise. Suppose, for example, an examination is intended to measure the amount of progress a student has made against a past performance or the degree to which a student is fulfilling his potential as measured by independent testing. Under these circumstances, essentially similar exams might receive very different grades. Similar exams could now be variously evaluated and still be evaluated fairly. This is further indication that it is fidelity to the evaluation process, and not logical consistency, that underlies our reflections on the fairness of such evaluations.

Let me try one final example to see if we can resurrect some normative importance for the notion of formal equality and link it to the concept of fairness. Imagine that a mother suddenly and arbitrarily gives five dollars to one of her two identical twins. Intuitively, we might think that the she should give the same amount of money to the second twin and, in the absence of justifying reasons, it would be unfair if she did not do so. One way to vindicate this intuition is to argue that logical consistency dictates that the mother should treat her children similarly, and the wrong resulting from her failure to do so is properly understood as an unfairness. But there is no apparent rule to follow here; nor does it seem that the principals involved have personal reasons for defecting from some social practice in which they participate.

Now, this case is similar to the panhandler situation, and if it is correct to insist that arbitrary acts of kindness do not set precedent that must be followed in the future on pain of contradiction (generating an unfairness), then we should conclude that the second twin has not been treated unfairly if the mother does not give him five dollars as well. But the two cases also differ in important respects. The mother bears an obvious and important relation to her children that is clearly lacking in the panhandler example. This relation is not simply biological; it has social dimensions also. The mother and her children belong to a family (and may even constitute a family) and therefore must be sensitive to all the responsibilities and concerns that we believe (given our social beliefs about family life) family members owe to and should have for one another. That is, the mother's position as mother matters. She is responsible for making sure that her children develop a healthy sense of self-respect and that they mature as individuals without loss of self-esteem.

She must also understand that she is a significant figure in their lives and her treatment of them will do much to help shape their sense of self. Of course, she must also do her part to keep the family together and work to sustain a healthy and nurturing home environment, an environment without jealousy and contempt and where perhaps unavoidable sibling rivalry is kept to a minimum. Even if her natural love and concern for her second twin is not sufficient to want her to make sure the child is not hurt by being overlooked by her mother, or made to feel left out or less cared for--a desire that would automatically incline her to give a similar amount of money to the second twin, her sense of responsibility as a mother should incline her to want to avoid causing the second twin to suffer in some such way.

The overlooked twin might reasonably react to the situation by insisting that things are unfair because his sibling got five dollars and he did not. The pain and disappointment underlying this complaint, however, will likely have little to do with the notion of fairness. The complaint, rather, will likely betray the child's concern that he is not loved as much as his sibling or that he does not receive the same care and concern from his mother that his sibling enjoys. It is the hurt associated with the feeling of being less cared for, coupled with the mother's apparent lack of concern for how her whimsical actions affect the sensitivities of her two children, that are cause for moral concern under the circumstances. There is, to be sure, a blemish here; the mother's apparent disregard for the feelings of both her children is objectionable. It is, then, generically unfair of her not to have more concern for both her children.

But is there anything unfair (in the specific, moral sense) going on here? This is a tricky question. It introduces a concern about a particular material element of fairness over which there may be reasonable disagreement. I have suggested that the mother's particular failing has to do with her inattentiveness to the well-being of both her children, and not with some abstract failure to treat equals equally. We might see this as unfair if we take fairness to involve fidelity to social practice and contend that the mother has failed to discharge her familial responsibilities effectively. But it is not clear that familial life is the type of social practice that typically houses such fairness concerns. The ties that unite family members seem more intimate, more personal, than the responsibilities we ordinarily associate with the concerns of fairness. So, while the mother's insensitivity to her child's feelings is surely objectionable and certainly wrong, it is less clear that we should consider it a type of unfairness.

Presumptive Equality

It seems, then, that we cannot understand the formal element of fairness in terms of logical consistency or formal equality. But perhaps we can make some progress here by calling the notion of presumptive equality onto center stage. According to the ideal of presumptive equality, all persons should be treated with equal care and concern unless there are justifiable moral reasons for unequal or dissimilar treatment (Katzner, 1971: pp. 253-58; Griffen, 1985: p. 113). Can such a notion supply the normative force required to drive the principle of fairness?

It is important to be clear on the moral character and logical implications of presumptive equality. If presumptive equality is taken to mean only that persons are, in fact, persons and should therefore be treated similarly, it quickly reduces to the notion of formal equality. The fact of personness, under this interpretation, merely establishes a relevant similarity that logically requires equal treatment unless differences are present that justify differential treatment. Once again, equally terrible treatment would satisfy this form of equality, and additionally, just about any difference between persons could possibly count as a relevant reason for dissimilar treatment. If presumptive equality is to serve the needs of the principle of fairness, then, there must be something more to it than this.

The requisite "something more" involves a moral claim about the need to treat people as significant equals rather than a claim about logical consistency. Supporters of presumptive equality suppose there is something of moral importance about being a human being. Kant's famous assertion that persons are creatures of incomparable worth serves this purpose and sets the precedent for those contemporary philosophers who insist that persons deserve equal concern and respect. The basis of this moral claim lies in the view that persons are independent, autonomous (and hence self-determining), and valuing beings--ends in themselves in Kantian jargon.

The moral belief that persons deserve concern and respect establishes an egalitarian ideal that would seem to support claims of presumptive equality. *All* persons deserve concern and respect, and because all persons matter as such, each person deserves the same concern and respect owed to others. Moreover, it is wrong to deviate from this moral imperative, and that is an end to the matter. In situations where deviation results in a morally unjustifiable inequality of treatment, we might want to say that the moral wrong on display involves an unfairness. And we might want to explain this by making appeal to the notion of Kantian fairness. From the standpoint of Kantian fairness, viz., the requirement to treat others with equal concern and respect, unjustifiable inequalities invariably involve a failure to treat someone with the proper respect, and so they must be considered unfair.

Since Kantian fairness seems to give precise expression to the ideal of presumptive equality, perhaps we can use it to make sense of the principle of fairness. An argument to this effect might go as follows. To benefit from the efforts of others without contributing one's fair share is a form of expropriation. When the labor and efforts of others enrich one's own life without proper compensation, the other is treated as a mere instrument for the development and promotion of one's own well-being. This, as Daniel Sullivan has said, "is to use and manipulate other persons and their efforts for one's own end" (1975: p. 328). Such expropriation need not be planned or deliberate, of course; the free-rider need not have schemed and plotted in order to get others to provide some service for him. Nonetheless, free-riding seems wrong, under the standard introduced by Kantian fairness, because it is deeply inegalitarian; it fails to accord those who have labored to bring about a collective benefit the respect they deserve as persons. So then, insofar as the principle of fairness erects a moral barrier against such unjustifiable expropriation, it might be defended by insisting that it merely articulates the demands of Kantian fairness.

The argument, however, falls into absurdity rather quickly. If Kantian fairness underwrites the principle of fairness, there can be no exceptions to the fair share requirement articulated by the principle. Anyone who enjoys a collective benefit as a result of the cooperative efforts of others must contribute her or his share to the enterprise. The principle of fairness now becomes uncompromising because the standards introduced by Kantian fairness hold unequivocally for all persons in all circumstances. That is, they hold for and against all persons as such and without qualification. But this is almost certainly too strong. While the argument might persuade us that the principle of fairness holds in those cases of deliberate non-involvement discussed above, there are still other cases where it seems to produce a wrong result. Sometimes, for example, unintended beneficiaries profit from the cooperative efforts of others simply because the cooperators cannot control the reach of their benefits. In many such cases we do not think this to be unfair. During the cold war, Canadians undoubtedly received a degree of security because they stood under the United State's umbrella of nuclear deterrence. But we could hardly insist that Canadians should assume a portion of the cost of the American defense budget for these years.

This *reductio* can be avoided if we claim that there is something about citizenship that matters. If we suppose that Canadians did benefit from standing under the American nuclear umbrella, we might still suppose that they are not free-riding because they are unintended beneficiaries falling outside the group whose members built the nuclear arsenal for their own protection. This seems right; here is a case where a group's willingness to pursue a particular collective good makes its members happy to bear the cost even though other parties may benefit as a result. And there does not appear to be anything unfair about this. But the principle of fairness, backed by Kantian fairness, will not permit this conclusion. Presumptive equality and the concerns of Kantian fairness that ride with it see only persons; they look through the contingencies of nationality, citizenship, culture, and the like, and focus exclusively on autonomous persons as morally relevant units.

In this regard, the principle of fairness as backed by Kantian fairness is uncompromising. It is wrong for *anyone* to benefit from the collective efforts of others without doing her or his share to bring about the benefit, and that is an end to the matter. Since receipt of benefit from a cooperative scheme without making proper restitution qualifies as a form of expropriation, it is morally objectionable. There simply are no morally relevant reasons that would justify such "free-riding."

It is easy to imagine still other apparent limitations upon the reach of the principle of fairness that cannot be accounted for if we see the principle as a formalized expression of Kantian fairness. Sometimes volunteer groups undertake cooperative projects specifically designed to benefit others simply because their members want to do good works. Volunteer groups often gather to pick up trash on the local beaches, for example, and it is fair to say that all beach users benefit from their cooperative efforts. Yet I doubt anyone would want to insist that all beach users have an obligation, under the principle of fairness, to join the clean-up effort or desist from using the beach in the future.

Moreover, sometimes an efficient division of labor, or the need for some expertise, determines who should labor to bring about some collective good. The family kitchen might not be big enough to allow all family members to help prepare the holiday meal, but few would insist that it is unfair to permit those who were unable to join in the preparation to enjoy the food, even though the food is clearly an excludable good. Nor is it reasonable to think that those who are excluded from the kitchen because they can't cook should also be barred from the table.

Sometimes too a lesser assumption of a burden does not mean that one can fairly be accorded a correspondingly lesser share of the good in question. People do not contribute equally to national security or police protection, but this is not reason to think it unfair if government supplies the same amount of protection or security to all citizens.[3] Perhaps this point reaches only the question of the proper ratio of burden to benefit required by the principle of fairness. But at the very least, it suggests that no specific ratio can be easily or straightforwardly attached to the principle of fairness. It seems then that receiving a benefit without assuming a corresponding burden, or a particular portion of the burden, is not always free-riding; sometimes, as in the case of unintended beneficiaries, one is just lucky; and sometimes this is just the way things go in a social setting where people contribute to the lives of others in differing ways--sometimes voluntary, sometimes compensated, sometimes loving or friendly.

So there is reason to reject the principle of fairness if it is backed by the notion of Kantian fairness. But the outright rejection of the principle also seems too strong. For there are occasions where the principle of fairness, or something like it, seems to be operative. If all members of the orchestra do their part to assure that the concert is a hit, the conductor cannot fairly applaud only the trombone section. If none of the players on the baseball team carry out their assignments properly, the manager cannot fairly blame only the pitcher for the team's loss. If all Jones's fellow neighbors join in a neighborhood crime watch program and keep an eye on Jones's house, Jones should, in all fairness, join in the activity also and help keep an eye on his neighbors' houses. In short, there seems to be *something* right about Rawls's insistence that "We are not to gain from the cooperative labors of others without doing our fair share" (Rawls, 1971: p. 112).

There is, then, reason to defend a weaker version of the principle. To do so, we must come to understand when the principle applies and when it does not. More specifically, we need to get clear on the circumstances under which fairness concerns come into play and trigger the normative convictions articulated by the principle. And we need to understand why the principle has legitimate normative force in these circumstances and why it lacks this force in other circumstances.

Fairness and Associative Attachments

Those situations in which the principle of fairness seems to have legitimate force have a common feature. The individuals involved are all linked to one another as fellow participants in some social practice or activity, i.e., they are linked as team members, orchestra members, neighbors, or citizens. From the standpoint of fairness, these linkages seem to count. In some of those cases where the principle does not seem to work there are no apparent associative linkages. Canadians are not linked to Americans in any manner that seems relevant to the pursuit of American national security, and consequently, it hardly makes sense to suppose that Canadians should contribute to American national security, even if they are unintended beneficiaries of American security efforts. But Americans are linked together, and so it makes sense to think that it is fair for Americans to share the cost of their national security, even if it is not fair that they all pay the same amount for this security.

Similarly, beach users do not seem linked in a manner that triggers fairness concerns. People should clean up after themselves when they use public places, to be sure; they should leave public spaces much as they found them so others can enjoy them. This matter of etiquette is surely of some importance. The failure to observe this etiquette constitutes a blemish that is objectionable. So we can say with confidence that people who leave their trash on the beach and don't bother to pick up after themselves are behaving unfairly in the generic sense. But I doubt that we could criticize them for being unfair, morally speaking, if they use the beach, fail to clean up the mess they make, and refuse to join voluntary clean-up crews dedicated to keeping the beach usable and attractive. We may properly criticize them for being rude, inconsiderate, and insensitive to the concerns of others, but this seems to be some distance from thinking that their conduct is somehow unfair. Beach use is simply much to diffuse an activity to qualify as a social practice one engages in *with* others. Here interpersonal linkages are a matter of proximity only.

In other cases where the principle does not seem to work, people are linked together, but in ways that permit them to work out divisions of labor, or to avail themselves of expertise. If family tradition allows the men to watch football on television while the women prepare the holiday meal, the family will not think this unfair, even though the men benefit from the efforts of the women without pulling their own weight. There will be those who think this really is unfair, and insist that if the men do not help in the kitchen, they should not be permitted to enjoy the meal. But it is the material element of fairness that is the focus of disagreement here. If family tradition determines the roles family members are to play and the responsibilities they are to have, differing traditions may assign roles and responsibilities differently. Viewed from inside one family tradition, or from a particular perspective on how familial division of labor ought to operate, the traditions of another family may seem unfair. And here the parties involved could agree on what fairness involves (i.e, on its formal element) and still disagree on whether a family practice displayed an unfairness (i.e., on its material element).

If these observations are right, then the principle of fairness is operative only where a particular type of linkage between people is present (Cf. Greenawalt, 1987: pp. 131-34). Free-riding becomes problematic, or rather benefitting from some cooperative enterprise without making a contribution becomes free-riding, only where it is possible to recognize some associative attachment or identification that links the free-rider to those providing the benefit. The free-rider fails to fulfill the expectations others have of him because of his attachments to them. Moreover, the nature of the attachment establishes what we can rightfully expect of the individuals linked together in some common enterprise. Neighbors, we can suppose, have a common interest in the security and beauty of the neighborhood. If the members of some neighborhood decide to pursue this common interest by initiating a neighborhood crime watch program that will benefit all neighbors, then each neighbor should, in all fairness, join in the process even if some of them were initially opposed to it.

Things are different, however, if the neighbors decide they want to establish a neighborhood softball team and build a field in a vacant lot so they can play. It seems wrong to think that a neighbor has any obligation, based upon fairness to help build the field or join the team, even if the construction of the field results in an increase in the value of his property. The difference here depends upon what is required of one as a neighbor, or upon the nature of the practice that forms the associative link between these people. Taking care in the security of the neighborhood is the neighborly thing to do, and when neighbors organize themselves in order to maximize this activity, fairness necessitates cooperation. But softball extra-curriculars have little to do with neighborliness, and so there seems nothing unfair about choosing not to participate in such an activity, even if one benefits from the decision of others to bring their home field into being.

If, on the other hand, I am wrong about the nature of neighborliness, if (perhaps) the notion of neighborliness has atrophied to such an extent that it no longer makes sense to think that neighbors have a common concern for the security of the neighborhood, then it would not be unfair if a neighbor benefitted from the crime watch program initiated by others without participating in kind. For now the required linkage is not present, and therefore, fairness is not an issue. Once again, however, this judgment goes to the material element of fairness. We can, that is, wonder whether the pertinent factors are present in our understanding of neighborliness to indicate the types of linkages that implicate fairness concerns without wondering about the nature of fairness. Thus we could be agreed on the meaning of fairness and still disagree on whether a person who refused to watch his neighbors' houses, knowing full well that they are keeping an eye on his, is being unfair.[4]

All this sheds some light on the normative force that seems to drive the principle of fairness. Fairness, it seems, has to do with what we owe others because we are socially linked to them in some pertinent manner and what we do not owe others because we are independent from them. This, in turn, suggests the problem with thinking of the fair distribution of burdens and benefits in terms of mathematical ratios and the arbitrary requirements of proportional equality. For the nature of one's share of the burden, along with the amount of benefit to be enjoyed, is most likely a consequence of the nature of the associative relationships constitutive of the cooperative activity in question. If two people are to share a cake, it is not always fair to simply divide the cake in half, a point I will discuss more fully momentarily. For present, it is sufficient to note that there is simply too much background information about the relation of the parties to the distribution and the particularities of their circumstances to hurry to such an arbitrary conclusion. Because fairness concerns arise within the context of associative attachments, they are simply too nuanced and too variegated to be reduced to crude formulae.

Among other things, this conclusion permits us to recognize some value in the claims of fairness made by Broad and Rawls and also to find some merit in Nozick's objections to the principle of fairness. If Rawls implicitly presumes some pertinent associative attachments in his use of the principle, Nozick explicitly appeals to situations where these attachments are lacking or uncertain. And we can now see that in cases where relevant associative linkages are present, the principle of fairness holds regardless of the consent of those who benefit from the cooperative efforts of their fellows. Correspondingly, where these linkages are not present, the principle of fairness does not reach beneficiaries who have opted not to participate in some cooperative scheme.

We might capture and articulate the associative nature of fairness concerns by appeal to either the notion of "adherence to rule" or "fidelity to social practice," both of which were introduced in the previous chapter. The first possibility, however, seems too narrow since it is possible that some of the associative links that might trigger fairness concerns do not involve explicit systems of rules. There seem to be few (if any) specific rules associated with the practice of neighborliness, for example. But the second possibility seems overly broad since not all social practices give rise to the type of fairness concerns that seem to direct the principle of fairness. It is necessary, then, to look more closely at both these possibilities to see if the notion of "adherence to rule" can be expanded to meet our needs or if the idea of "fidelity to social practice" can be suitably qualified.

Notes

1. Few problems present themselves in the case of excludable goods. If a person opts out of a cooperative scheme involving excludable goods, she simply does not receive a share of the benefit. If goods are excludable and she takes a share in spite of her refusal to participate (i.e., if she refuses to be excluded), we can suppose she has reversed her decision not to participate and now owes her share of the burden.

2. Perhaps someone might want to insist that equally horrible treatment is wrong but if it is really equal it is still fair. To hold such a view, one must insist with a vengeance that fairness is a fundamentally comparative notion. I doubt, however, that we would think terrible but equal treatment as at least having the virtue of being fair. The point, moreover, is not that the fairness of such equal treatment is insignificant from a moral point of view; instead, the point is that there is nothing fair going on here. Fairness simply does not require that we do something wrong in order to sustain a formal equality of treatment.

3. It does seem unfair, however, if a citizen does not contribute something, or as best he can, to national security. Yet contribution is unrelated to the benefit received. Some citizens will pay far more for national security than will others, even though all receive the same amount of security; and yet, this does not seem unfair provided the taxing policy employed by the state qualifies as fair. Nor can this asymmetry be easily explained by appeal to the relative benefits gained by maintaining national security. The person who pays more for national security might be better off if another state conquered his home state, while the person who pays less for this security might be worse off if the change were made.

Yet citizenship still matters in our reflections about the fair cost of national security. A Canadian living close to the border of the United States may receive the same security against, say, Russian aggression against North America as an American does living just across the border, thanks to American nuclear deterrence. Yet fairness still does not seem to require the Canadian to pay his share of the cost of the security gains from the American arsenal, while fairness does seem to require the American to pay something in this direction.

4. Neighborhoods that undertake extra-neighborly activities sometimes insist that new neighbors join in the activities by requiring them to sign restrictive covenants. This practice generates obligations based upon consent rather than upon the common expectations of being neighborly. Since the notion of neighborliness seems to be in atrophy, particularly in larger urban and more modern suburban "communities" the linkages that once tied neighbors together, and constituted the formal practice of being neighborly, are now in jeopardy. The loss may be unfortunate, but more importantly for my objectives here, it may also make my examples more controversial.

Chapter Four

Fairness and Following Rules

Two possible ways to account for the formal element of fairness have emerged from the discussion thus far: Adherence to rule and fidelity to social practice. I want now to consider the first of these. There are two reasons to think that fairness can be profitably analyzed in terms of adherence to rule. First, when people break the rules of play to advantage themselves, they are cheating and this is unfair. By parity of reason, then, sticking to the rules would seem to be fair. Secondly, we have also noticed that fairness seems to be implicated when we worry about the comparatively equal treatment of persons. But to make sense of this, we also noticed, we must have recourse to some rule that dictates how people are to be treated. So again, it looks as if fairness is achieved only if the proper rule is followed.

Nevertheless, this view has several problems. As we shall see, there are at least three reasons why we cannot get very far by trying to understand fairness in terms of adherence to rule. First, rules and procedures are themselves subject to fairness critiques. Second, adherence to legitimate rules can occasionally result in an unfairness, and third, we sometimes worry about the fairness of social activities that do not appear to be governed by fixed rules.

Fairness and Formal Justice

As things stand, the notion of adherence to rule is too uncertain to be of much use in understanding the concept of fairness. There are many different types of rules that constitute and regulate social activities in diverse ways, and not all of these generate fairness concerns (Cf. Black, 1962: pp. 95-133; Schauer, 1991: pp. 12-16). A rule like "Roses should be pruned in late February" offers good advice to gardeners, but it offers advice only. Gardeners who fail to prune their roses in late February may be negligent, but it would be silly to say they have been gardening unfairly. On the other hand, a rule like "Promises ought to be kept" offers a more commanding guide to conduct. A person who fails to adhere to this rule, and who breaks a promise without justificatory reasons for doing so, has done something wrong. But the wrong on display has nothing to do with being unfair, and we do not ordinarily think that a person's dedication to keeping her promises is an indicator of fairmindedness.

So it is necessary to specify the types of rules, or rule following situations, that do seem to implicate fairness concerns. A generalized account of such rules, abstracted from the material elements of fairness and unfairness encountered thus far, would go as follows: Fairness involves adherence to those prescriptive rules that regulate, govern, organize, and/or control some rule-based associative practice or activity. This locates the concerns of fairness within specific associative practices, viz., those possessing prescriptive rules for the control of associative activities, and consequently confines fairness judgments to evaluations of the legitimacy or propriety of one's play or participation, as measured against the official requirements of the rules. The rules of play that govern competitive events, like athletic contests and admissions programs, are comprehended by this account. But so too are more generalized maxims like, "first come, first served," when they are embedded in more general distributive practices.

Thinking of fairness in terms of adherence to rule again calls to mind the concept of formal justice which is often understood in similar terms (Cf. Perelman, 1963: pp. 36-45). But there is a fairly standard objection to thinking of justice this way. If some rule, R, makes p appropriate treatment for any subject who is an x, then justice is done when R is followed. Following R guarantees that S gets her just deserts, if S is an x. Justice is done, however, because S_x gets p (where p = that which is deserved under R), i.e., because R is followed, and not because of adherence to the meta-rule, J, which stipulates that justice requires adherence to rules like R. Strictly speaking, justice does not *require* adherence to rule; it requires that people get their just deserts whether or not this is specified by rule. Reference to adherence to rule merely describes what occurs when some rule specifying one's just deserts is followed. And this, of course, indicates that we cannot hope to understand justice formally as adherence to rule; for to do so confuses consequence with condition (Cf. Carr, 1981: pp. 212-17).

We might now simply re-issue this argument to defeat the claim that fairness is understandable in terms of adherence to rule. This would be appropriate, however, only if justice and fairness are equivalent concepts, and at the moment we have no reason to think this is so. But since we also have no reason to think this is not so, we had best look into the matter further.

Justice, I have suggested, is concerned with the receipt of just deserts. Is fairness also concerned with this? An affirmative answer to this question would not justify the conclusion that fairness and justice are conceptual equivalents. Receipt of just deserts, for example, may be a material element of fairness, but there might be more to fairness than this. (There might be more to the concept of justice as well, but for present purposes I will ignore this possibility.) But there is no reason to worry about this since it does not seem that fairness has much to do with the receipt of just deserts.

Let me try to tease out the conceptual differences here with the aid of a simple example. Suppose S receives a punishment she does not deserve, perhaps because she is wrongly convicted of a crime she did not commit. This is reason to think that S has been done an injustice. But has she also been treated unfairly? Granted, S may claim that her punishment is unfair. This could mean, and I think it frequently does mean, that S is insisting that her punishment is improper, wrong, or even unjust--and hence generically unfair. But she could mean something more specific; she could mean that her punishment is unfair, morally speaking, because it is undeserved. It would be foolhardy to deny that people occasionally speak this way, i.e., in a manner that equates fairness with justice. Yet this merely introduces a confusion that obscures the subtle conceptual difference between fairness and justice.

Imagine that S's unfortunate conviction follows a trial that qualifies as fair and that she is sentenced to a punishment commensurate with the nature of the crime she is mistakenly said to have committed. In this case, S's punishment is unjust, in a sense, but I don't think we can also say that she is being punished unfairly.[1] The claim of injustice is appropriate because S does not deserve to be punished since she has done nothing wrong (in fact, S's innocence means that she deserves not to be punished). Concerns for the fairness of her treatment, on the other hand, focus exclusively on process in this situation rather than on questions of desert. If proper procedures were followed during her criminal prosecution, and if the punishment meted out is appropriate to her alleged crime, there is little room for her to claim that she has been dealt with unfairly. Justice has not been done, we must conclude, even though the trial was fair.

Imagine, however, that S is sentenced, say, to a punishment far too severe for the crime she allegedly committed, perhaps because the judge happens to dislike her. Now she could justifiably complain about both the justness and the fairness of her treatment. In fact she now seems to suffer a double injustice. Since she did not commit the crime for which she has been found guilty, any punishment is undeserved--and hence unjust. But too, since the punishment assigned her is more severe than what she putatively deserves, given the nature of her alleged crime, it too is undeserved--and hence unjust. In the latter case, the concerns of justice appear to overlap the concerns of fairness, but it is important to see that they are not the same. For justice looks only to the question of desert; given the nature of the crime S has been convicted of, her assigned punishment is undeserved because too severe.

Fairness, however, looks to the integrity of process and not to desert. According to the balance we expect between crime and punishment, S's punishment is too severe. Something has gone wrong--perhaps, again, the judge deviated from proper procedures for inappropriate reasons. And this deviation from the proper standards of criminal procedure is unfair. It is not, however, the punishment that is unfair, although it is the punishment that is unjust. Rather the *sentencing* is unfair, i.e., S has been sentenced unfairly. In the example at hand, this has led to an injustice. So, S can complain about the justness of her punishment by pointing to the unfairness of her sentencing. Doing so would probably not do her much good, but at least we could say that she understands the conceptual differences between justice and fairness.

Since the concepts of justice and fairness are not equivalent, at least with regard to their formal elements, we cannot repeat the objection to understanding formal justice in terms of adherence to rule when we turn to the concept of fairness. And because fairness seems concerned with procedural integrity, at least in the example at hand, it still looks as if it might be possible to understand fairness in these terms. There is, accordingly, reason to consider it further.

Procedural and Background Fairness

While at times it seems that fairness involves something like adherence to rule, there are several reasons to think that we cannot make sense of the concept's formal element this way. For one thing, sometimes we worry about the fairness of certain rules and procedures themselves. We do so in order to review the way these rules contribute to, advance, or generally facilitate the underlying purpose or point of the practice they regulate.

The so-called "fair trial doctrine" that characterized the general approach to criminal justice litigation assumed by the United States Supreme Court prior to the 1960s provides an apt illustration of this general point (Cf. Palko v. Connecticut, 302 US 319, (1937)). The Justices supportive of the fair trial doctrine were of the opinion that some state criminal justice procedures could satisfy the ideals of due process even if they did not correspond exactly to the federal construction of due process as outlined by the Fourth, Fifth, and Sixth Amendments to the Constitution of the United States. States were thus allowed to construct their own rules for criminal prosecution, and when asked to review the propriety of state criminal justice proceedings, the Court evaluated the basic fairness of the criminal process rather than whether the process followed the rules of the federal Constitution. The process was considered fair, in turn, if the Court concluded that it was faithful to the spirit of due process of law, viz., the ideals of adversarialness and presumption of innocence.

It may be worthwhile to dwell on this point for a moment in order to be clear on what is at issue. There may be a number of different rule systems that correspond to the spirit of due process of law. If so, the federal model of criminal justice would not be the only model that would meet due process requirements, and states could conceivably adopt alternatives that happen to work just as well. If we suppose that this is the case, the Court could have been concerned, in weighing the fairness of a criminal prosecution, to see if state procedures were followed by state courts, assuming state procedures involved a legitimate but constitutionally distinct method for assuring due process. But this is not what the Court was doing.[2] Instead, its review focused on whether state procedures, as applied in the particular case under review, satisfied standards of fundamental fairness. And recourse to fairness here seems understandable only in terms of fidelity to the spirit of due process. In short, the state rules and procedures were themselves the target of review, and the standard of review involved some sense of the fairness of the criminal process that was independent of, and prior to, the rules and procedures challenged in the litigation.

This objection calls to mind the familiar distinction between procedural and background fairness. It might seem, for example, that the Court simply invoked the considerations of background fairness to declare upon the procedural fairness of state processes. But I don't think there is much to be said for this distinction, and for reasons worth considering for a moment. Brian Barry describes the distinction as follows, "Procedural fairness rules out one boxer having a piece of lead inside his gloves, but background fairness would also rule out any undue disparity in the weight of the boxers; similarly background fairness would rule out sailing boats or cars of different sizes being raced against one another unless suitably handicapped"(1965: pp. 98-99).

Procedural fairness, then, looks to adherence to the prescriptive rules that regulate a particular activity. An event qualifies as procedurally fair, according to Barry, if and when it is conducted in conformity with the requisite prescriptive rules. A boxer who puts a piece of lead inside his glove is being procedurally unfair because the rules do not permit him to do this. Such a transgression is a form of cheating, but the transgression itself constitutes the unfairness.

Background fairness, on the other hand, looks to the construction of the contest itself to determine whether the prescriptive rules permit a true or viable test of the skill or talent it is intended to measure. As Barry explains, "The criteria of background fairness . . . vary according to the 'right result.' If all that is being tested is the ability to knock out an opponent, there is no need for any limits on the disparity of size between boxers; but if the boxing match is supposed to be a test of skill, 'background fairness' must be brought in to specify the maximum disparity beyond which skill is secondary in determining the result to brute force" (1965: p. 103). So, procedural rules that set the standards of play may be judged unfair according to the standards of background fairness if they obscure or are inconsistent with the realization of the "right result."

But no sooner is the distinction stated than it fades away like the notorious Cheshire Cat. The problem is that the notion of procedural fairness has no independent force or validity; there is simply no place here for a concept to go. Rules and procedures may be fair or unfair when measured against background fairness. If unfair, they should be amended; if fair, they should be followed. And it is always fair to follow a fair rule, but not because one is following a rule. That is, it is fair to follow a fair rule because the rule is fair and not because it is a rule. The background conditions that establish the fairness of the rule also establish the fairness of adhering to the rule. To get things right, then, we must pull the notion of background fairness into the foreground, and once we do this, there is no longer a point to the distinction.

The rules that are constitutive and regulative of certain social practices cannot be considered arbitrary or independently variable. The rules themselves must serve an important purpose. They do something more than merely regulate participation in the event they govern. They also enable the determination of what Barry calls the "right result." Boxing is a type of contest that measures pugilistic skills and excellence. For such a measure to be possible, however, regulatory rules are required to standardize and govern the process in a manner that enables the skill and ability we value to excel. Such a test of skill requires, as Barry rightly notes, that independent variables which might defeat the test be controlled. So, weight classes help promote the test of pugilistic excellence by guaranteeing that a bigger and stronger pugilist will not defeat a smaller boxer by means of pure brawn alone. But similarly, putting lead in a boxer's gloves will artificially increase the damage his blows will do, and this distorts the test of excellence as well. The problem with putting lead in one's boxing gloves, then, is not that it violates a rule--which it does--but that it disrupts the nature of the contest. *This* is why it is unfair, and *this* is why it is prohibited by rule.

Sometimes, it seems that procedural fairness is important because it checks against the possibility that one contestant will achieve an unfair advantage. A boxer who manages to put lead in his gloves before his match would seem to have such an advantage. But the unfairness here is not the result either of a breach of procedure or the gaining of an illicit advantage. (The lead may actually even up the respective chances of winning if one's opponent is a far superior pugilist.) Instead, the unfairness results because the lead endangers the integrity of the contest. Now a well-placed blow could do greater damage than it normally would and perhaps determine the outcome of the contest. The lead increases the punching power of one contestant, but it does so in a manner inconsistent with the test of skill that is the telos of the competition. Notice here that things would be no fairer if *both* boxers had lead in their gloves. While the increase in punching power is now roughly equal between the two boxers, it is still likely that a lucky punch will determine the outcome of the contest rather than the respective skills of the two boxers. This, once again, defeats the likelihood that the contest will have a "right result."

Sometimes the rules create (or constitute) the skill we value. Shooting a basketball well, for example, is controlled by the fact that the basket is ten feet off the ground, as set by rule. Shooting a basketball well would involve something different if the basket was four feet, or twenty feet, off the ground. At other times, the rules harness and refine the skill we value. This seems to be the case with regard to boxing, where the skills of the pugilist are refined by rules that separate boxers from brawlers. In either case, the rules put into effect, so to speak, the skills being tested, and their fairness depends upon their success in constructing and controlling an activity intended to highlight these skills.

So then, the fairness of the prescriptive rules that regulate and govern some event or practice apparently depends upon the way these rules facilitate the spirit, ideals, purpose, or point that underlies and inspires the event itself; they rely, that is, on the way these rules promote the end, or telos, of the practice they govern. If it is unfair for a boxer to put lead in his gloves, it must be because allowing this is inconsistent with the point or purpose of the competition itself. There is no true competition, no real test of pugilistic skill, if a boxer takes such liberties, perhaps because he cares more about winning than about having a "fair fight." Similarly, a criminal trial that serves only as an excuse for a lynching is hardly fair because it fails to serve the purpose that explains why those accused of criminal activity are required to stand before the bar of justice. And this is some indication that the formal element of fairness is more profitably understood in terms of fidelity to the telos, objective, or ideals--to the pursuit of the "right result"--of some social practice than in terms of adherence to rule.

Following Rules and Acting Unfairly

There is a second, albeit related, objection to thinking of fairness in terms of adherence to prescriptive rules which trades on the fact that adherence to otherwise fair rules seems at times to be unfair. Rawls has provided a cogent statement of the point behind this objection:

> Usually acting unfairly is not so much the breaking of any particular rule, even if the infraction is difficult to detect (cheating), but taking advantage of loop-holes or ambiguities in rules, availing oneself of unexpected or special circumstances which make it impossible to enforce them, insisting that rules be enforced to one's advantage when they should be suspended, and more generally, acting contrary to the intention of the practice (1958: p. 180).

Here Rawls draws attention to the fact that rules can sometimes be exploited in ways that work an unfairness and that sometimes (and somewhat remarkably) adherence to rules can actually result in an unfairness. He also suggests that being fair involves something like fidelity to the "intention of the practice" within which fairness concerns arise when this "intention" requires deviation from or suspension of the prescriptive rules of the practice.

Now, it is not difficult to see that sometimes a strict adherence to otherwise fair rules can be unfair. This happens, for example, in situations where rules that are customarily ignored, or loosely interpreted, are suddenly enforced or strictly interpreted. To illustrate, consider the rule against the illegal use of hands ("holding") in American football. It is prohibited by rule for offensive players to use their hands while blocking for the ball carrier, and yet football players, television commentators, and almost all mildly knowledgeable spectators know that holding actually occurs on almost every play. Imagine, then, a scenario where officials call a holding penalty against a player at a crucial moment of the game, even though they have not previously penalized this same infraction, and for the same type of "illegal" block, during the course of play. While we can suppose that the block really did involve an illegal use of hands, and hence that the official's call is just, there still seems to be something unfair (and not just generically unfair) going on here. How might we account for this?

Perhaps we can answer this question by recurring to our old friend, consistency. Might the consistent interpretation of the rules not work as a prerequisite for fairness? Coaches and athletes sometimes say, for example, that they care less about how the officials interpret and apply the rules than they do about the consistency of their calls. Players can adjust to the way the rules are interpreted, provided they are interpreted consistently, and play can then go forward.

But of course a consistent interpretation of the rules can still be unfair. Suppose officials know that interpreting the rules in a particular way will aid one team and disadvantage the other, and they have bet money on the team that will be advantaged. Further, rules cannot be interpreted in just any manner whatsoever. Some rules, as we have seen, literally create the activity they are designed to govern. If the rules are not interpreted in a manner faithful to the activity itself, the activity ceases to be a test of those skills it is intended to test. The point of the contest is thus lost in the process of rule interpretation. Consistency of interpretation, then, must be supplemented with some reference to the propriety of the interpretation applied by officials.

We might still wonder why consistency of interpretation should matter to participants in athletic contests. Consistent interpretations do not always mean that neither side is disadvantaged, even if the interpretation is not intended to favor one side. (Imagine an umpire calling pitches in a baseball game and employing a low strike zone, or a strike zone that does not recognize pitches "around the letters" as strikes. Suppose one team's pitcher likes to through low pitches while the other team's pitcher relies on high fastballs.) Nor do inconsistent interpretations mean that both sides will be disadvantaged, as is the case with the umpire who changes his interpretation of the strike zone each inning. Perhaps then we should say that consistency of interpretation is less important than the fairness of interpretation, assuming we can get clear on precisely what this means.

These comments merely repeat the general objection to linking consistency to fairness already discussed, and so the problems introduced here should not seem terribly surprising. There is another reason, however, why competitors may like to see athletic contests called consistently. Because competitors are able to adjust to the way the game is being officiated, if it is officiated consistently, they can be sure the contest is a true competition. They are now able to do their best within the context of play established by the officials. This may not provide them with their best chance of winning--they may be happier if the rules were interpreted more to their liking--but it guarantees that all contestants know what is going on and what is proper and what is improper play. Provided the rules are consistently applied, and provided their application is faithful to the spirit or telos of the competition, I think we must conclude that the contest is a fair one, even if one (or both) of the competitors would like to see the rules applied differently. For now the contest can be played in a manner that makes it a true test of the skill or talent it is intended to measure. This is all we can ask, and it is all fairness demands.[3]

Adherence to rule may also work an unfairness by permitting the exploitation of rules. This occurs when rule violations are worth the penalty they bring. Sometimes this is part of the game, as is the case in basketball where it might pay for the losing team to foul near the end of the game in order to make its opponent shoot (and make) foul shots. This is a last-ditch effort at winning and one that might work if one's opponent is not good at shooting foul shots.[4] More frequently, however, this involves unusual or unanticipated situations not easily accommodated by recourse to the standard rules of play.

To illustrate, consider an example inspired by actual events. Imagine a game of American football where a ball carrier has broken free from all the tacklers on the opposing team and is running down the sideline for a certain touchdown. Imagine now that he is running along his opponent's side of the field and a distraught member of the opposing team, who is not in the game at the moment, jumps from the bench and tackles the ball carrier. The resultant penalty for illegal participation involves a modest loss of yardage. Such a penalty is obviously worth the cost if it saves a touchdown (and perhaps prevents the other team from winning the game). Insisting that the rule be enforced, however, (rather than conceding the touchdown) seems positively unfair. And it does so because it is inconsistent with the competitive spirit of the event. If cheating is permitted to prosper, and if cheaters are awarded for their rule exploitation, what is the point of playing the game? A true test of skill and ability is no longer possible.

Can we breathe life back into the notion of adherence to rule by arguing that the problem of rule exploitation results from the vagueness or indeterminacy of rules? Perhaps the remedy for such situations is to guarantee fairness qua adherence to prescriptive rules by making rules more explicit, exact, and comprehensive. In the case of illegal participation in football, for example, we might add a codicil to the proper rule stipulating that a touchdown is to be awarded when a player comes off the bench to interfere with play in a manner that costs the opponent a certain touchdown.

Rule changes are frequently inspired by situations of this sort and rule books grow in response to those who are willing to exploit the rules in order to win. This is perhaps sad testimony to the fact that winning matters more to some than playing fairly. So, rules proliferate in the rather hopeless effort to stipulate precisely the requirements of fair play. But the effort really is hopeless for the most part. The uncertain and unimaginable nature of the way things often go in contested social practices like athletic competitions makes it virtually impossible to craft rules that are sufficiently specific to anticipate and account for all likely circumstances. It is simply not possible to govern such practices with a system of rules so detailed that all situations which might distort the "intention of the practice" are eliminated or controlled. Rules require officials to make judgments, and the more codicils we add, the more we simply change the nature of the judgments that must be made. What should we do, for example, if a player comes off the bench in a football game and tackles a ball carrier even if a teammate, properly in the game, could possibly have made the tackle farther down field?

It is also worth noting and emphasizing that fairness matters greatly in contested social practices precisely because it is not possible to legislate their fairness by means of a system of rules. Because the participants can be presumed to have some sense of the intention, or purpose, of the practice--some sense of what it is about or how it is supposed to go, they can understand what it means to play or participate fairly. Players, officials, and spectators alike can adjust to situations where a strict adherence to the rules will work an unfairness, and they can do so because they have an understanding of fairness that is independent of, and that informs, their understanding of the rules of play and the spirit or telos of the game. Without this underlying sense of fairness, the ability to realize the ends or objectives of those practices where fairness matters would be greatly jeopardized, if not entirely lost.

If winning was all that mattered, it would make perfect sense for players not in the game to interfere with play to prevent opponents from scoring. But winning is not all that matters; it is secondary to playing the game. It is remarkably unusual for sideline players to interfere with play, and if they do, it is even more unusual for coaches to insist that the rules be enforced such that they benefit from the interference. Where the rules are exploitable in such a manner that breaking them could work an advantage if the opponent cannot capitalize on the infraction (as in the case of basketball), it is good play to use the rules to one's advantage. If this seems unfair upon reflection, the rules can be changed to eliminate this practice. But this judgment again presumes a sense of fairness independent of the notion of adherence to rule. This is the very same sense of fairness required to underwrite our commitment to and interpretation of the rules of play. More importantly, it is the same sense of fairness necessary to be assured that the game will go well, or as it should. For to say that the game itself matters is to say that fair play matters; fair play evidences commitment to the game, to the talent or skill that it highlights, and to the pursuit of excellence it makes possible.

Fair Bargains and Bargaining Fairly

We now have several reasons to abandon efforts to understand fairness in terms of adherence to rule, but at the risk of seeming to flog a dead horse, I want to consider one more. Some contexts in which fairness concerns arise do not appear to be structured by rules, or the rules associated with them are so nebulous, so ethereal, that they defy easy characterization. The practice of bargaining offers an illustrative example. While it is probably correct to say that there is a right way to bargain, bargaining is not an activity governed and directed by explicit rules. Nonetheless, we speak of fair bargains and of bargaining fairly, and when we do, it is fairness that seems to be at issue.

To bargain is to enter a transaction process with another in which both parties seek to identify a point of agreement, involving some sort of mutual exchange, that both consider preferable to the status quo. The bargain is sealed if the parties succeed in reaching an agreement point and consequently commit to the mutual exchange. Bargainers presumably want to do as well for themselves as they can, i.e., to maximize their benefit comparative to their status quo, and for this reason bargaining is often supposed to be a type of contest with each bargainer chiefly concerned about maximizing her own situation and without regard for the situation of fellow bargainers. While bargaining might generate a cooperative interaction as an outcome, it is not, according to this view, a cooperative endeavor (Cf. Gauthier, 1986: p. 129). This raises an important question about the cooperative nature of bargaining.

Although bargaining does not seem to be governed by explicit prescriptive rules, it does constitute what I have called a contested social practice. The participants have personal interests at stake and personal reasons for preferring some outcomes to others that incline them to discount the interests of their fellow bargainers. Bargaining as a contested practice falls rather short of a state of war, however, if we understand a state of war to be a "win at all costs" situation.

Some find considerable wisdom in the old saw, "All is fair in love and war." This is, I suppose, a curious way of saying that fairness is not considered relevant to the pursuit of a loved one or the prosecution of a war. When it comes to such things, winning is all that matters. The stakes are so great that one can, and presumably should, do anything and everything in one's power to realize the desired outcome. This is, to be sure, something of an exaggeration. It would be wrong to kill a rival lover, for example, and perhaps even counter-productive. Moreover, I doubt anyone would think to try and put a happy spin on such conduct by insisting that at least it was not an unfair thing to do. From a moral point of view, we cannot do just anything to gain the hand of a loved one, but the moral constraints in operation here seem unrelated to fairness concerns.

Perhaps then it is only in warfare that we can say winning is all that matters. If so, this is a rather recent understanding of war, which was once viewed simply as an extension of politics by other means, as Clauswitz put it. Yet even if some general rules of engagement are acknowledged, warfare, like the pursuit of a lover, fails to qualify as a cooperative social practice, and this explains why fairness concerns do not arise in these situations.

Warfare lacks a shared purpose; that is, combatants in warfare are not doing something together. They are not joined by a common commitment to a cooperative enterprise. They are antagonists and that is an end to the matter. Each side seeks to promote its interests without regard for the interests of the opposition. Neither side has any particular interest in the courage, honor, or skill of its warriors. Although courage is a virtue of warfare, wars are not fought to test the strength or skill of competing warriors. This separates warfare (and the pursuit of a lover) from contests like boxing matches which, as we have seen, happen to have "right results." Boxing matches, that is, are purposive in a way that warfare is not; boxing matches are held in order to test skill and demonstrate pugilistic excellence. This is their point, their telos, and while this might not explain why the contestants enter the fray, it presumably guides and informs their sense of what they are doing. But warfare has no such telos, no such shared understanding; combatants seek only to achieve their own interests and realize their own ends. This is no place for fairness.

If we think bargaining is not a cooperative activity, we may prefer to consider it a free-for-all that qualifies as, or at least resembles, a state of war. Bargainers, this view goes, have no interest in the concerns of their adversaries and need have no such interest. Their sole concern is to advance their own well-being as best they can. Yet this view stands in tenuous juxtaposition to another prevalent view that suggests that bargains have "right results" or fair outcomes. For we do commonly speak of dealing, trading, and bargaining fairly, and here fairness judgments evaluate the process that takes place. If trading or bargaining actually resembles a state of war rather than a cooperative practice, then it is hard to see what sense such judgments could have.[5]

But we do make such judgments, and make them intelligibly, and this gives us reason to suppose that trading and bargaining are really cooperative practices and not states of war. For these judgments are understandable only if we suppose that bargaining (trading, dealing, etc.) is an associative practice in which the participants seek to discover a mutually acceptable point of agreement (or equilibrium point) for an exchange of goods or services.

Reference to mutuality in this account of bargaining signals a required commitment on the part of each bargainer to the point or telos of the activity. And this informs a specific sense of fair bargaining. To bargain fairly is to display honesty and openness in the process, to disclose fully all information pertinent to the process, to represent one's interests exactly, to make a sincere effort to achieve an equilibrium, and to dedicate oneself to the spirit of the exchange between bargainers. Someone who bargains but fails to meet these standards bargains unfairly. By putting oneself first, by hiding relevant information, by lying about one's situation, and so forth, a bargainer defeats the point of bargaining. Someone who does these things is not interested in achieving equilibrium; she is interested only in realizing her own personal interests without regard to the interests of those with whom she is joined as a fellow bargainer.

In this regard, bargaining resembles a type of rational discussion. Jon Elster, who wants to distinguish bargaining from rational discussion, claims that only the strength of argument matters in rational discussion while variations in bargaining power matter in bargaining situations (1989: p. 51). But it seems possible to allow some room for bargaining power and still insist that bargaining is a cooperative activity where fellow participants are dedicated to finding an acceptable equilibrium point. Discrepancies in bargaining power make some more willing to drive a hard bargain, or to hold out for an equilibrium point more advantageous to them than to fellow bargainers. Yet this does not seem to compromise a sense of fair bargaining provided hard bargainers make their position known and understandable.

Elster seems right to contend that bargaining situations take persons as they are and bargaining power as it is. Bargaining is not necessarily unfair simply because bargaining power is not roughly equal. (This issue will receive further consideration in Chapter Eight.) But inequalities in bargaining power do not mean that the bargaining process falls short of rational discussion. For reasoned discussion, in the face of these inequalities, is still a necessary condition of the bargaining process. And this means that bargainers must avoid deceit, trickery, bullying, and other forms of unfair bargaining in favor of a committed search for an equilibrium point.

Similarly, while we can speak of bargains having right results. The propriety of the result is determined by the willingness of bargainers to accept a proposed transaction that has been fairly bargained. It is not, therefore, knowable in principle prior to the bargaining process. This differs importantly from the view that right results depend primarily on the way the outcome distributes the comparative advantages of the bargainers. For example, D. D. Raphael, who holds a position like this, thinks that a right result is reached if a bargain yields a roughly equal advantaging, though he concedes possible troubles in measurement (1955: p. 64).

However, I fail to see why a fair bargain should require a roughly equal advantaging, or why the fairness of a bargain should be determined by the nature of its outcome. If P is happy with a fairly bargained agreement, even though he knows that Q, his bargaining partner, will benefit more than he will from the equilibrium point reached, why should the bargain qualify as unfair? Fair bargaining, then, does not mean working together to strike a perfectly equitable arrangement; in this regard, it does differ from a rational discussion inspired by an underlying ethic of egalitarianism. Bargaining leaves room for a bargainer to look to his own interests and try to do as well for himself as he can. And fair bargaining does not require a bargainer to regard his interests as equal to the interests of his bargaining partners. This too is a part of the ethics of bargaining. Each bargainer is responsible for looking out for his own interests, and one does not bargain unfairly if one does not warn one's partner that he is not sufficiently attentive to his own concerns.

Bargainers, like athletes, can play to win, but again like athletes, they cannot cheat in the process. They can work for the best deal possible, and they are free to settle when they think the terms properly acceptable or to disengage when they think no equilibrium point can be found. When it comes to bargaining, it is always possible to speak of "right results," but it is not always possible to know them independent of a fair bargaining process.

People tend to avoid bargaining with known swindlers because there is no point in dealing with such people. Similarly, fairly bargained outcomes are generally stable; when one is confident that equilibrium has been reached, there is little reason to defect from the bargain. Nevertheless, the ethic that informs the bargaining process cannot be properly regarded as a system of rules. While the ethic of fair bargaining identifies the right way to bargain, it is not readily articulated in a set of prescriptive rules that tells one how to bargain or that constitutes the bargaining process. And since this does not detract from our concern for the fairness of bargains, or from concerns about bargaining fairly, we cannot explain the formal element of fairness underlying these material elements in terms of adherence to prescriptive rules.

Notes

1. The reason for the qualification is that one's just deserts, in criminal law, may be determined only as a result of a fair trial. If one is convicted as the consequence of a fair trial, one deserves to be punished. Criminal prosecution, according to this view, is not concerned with the ideal of justice--getting things right every time, so to speak, but with adherence to proper procedures. Still, it is evident that criminal prosecution doesn't always "get it right" and some innocents will be punished for something they did not do. And in this light, we can say that they are treated in a way they do not deserve, i.e., they are treated unjustly.

2. The United States Supreme Court even lacks jurisdiction to review the propriety of state procedures according to state standards. This responsibility falls to state appellate courts.

3. As should be evident, this point illustrates why we might justifiably think that the official's holding call, in the above example, is unfair. Since the officials have not called holding against similar blocking techniques previously, players will reasonably assume that the technique being employed is generically fair. So, by making the block he makes, the player has reason to suppose he is making a (generically) fair block, i.e., he is playing fairly within the rules in order to aid his team. So, the player could not have known that his actions constituted a foul. He could have no reason not to make the block in the manner he did. Since a fair contest requires that the competitors know how to go about playing the game, the official's sudden and unexpected holding call now qualifies as unfair.

4. The fairness of this strategy, it is worth noting, remains a matter of controversy. In recent years, some rule changes have been introduced to penalize intentional fouling more severely in an attempt to deter the practice.

5. Even if we supposed that trading and bargaining could be only generically fair, we would still have a problem. We still need to understand what *this* judgment could mean. It registers a sense of propriety or legitimacy, to be sure. But what is the standard of propriety that permits even this weak expression? Why, that is, would one feel inclined to think that a process identifiable as a state of war could be minimally, or generically, fair or unfair?

Chapter Five

Fidelity to Social Practice

The argument so far suggests, but suggests only, that the formal element of fairness can be described most effectively by appeal to the idea of fidelity to social practice. Yet this remains an unhappily obscure and vague notion. Considerable theoretical refinement is necessary before it can provide satisfactory insight into the formal element of fairness. In particular, two key issues need to be addressed. First, we must clarify the meaning of "fidelity to social practice" and consider whether this notion can be shaped to cover successfully those contexts, and only those contexts, where fairness concerns evidently arise. Second, we need to see whether the notion of fidelity to social practice can capture and expose the normative character of fairness and thus explain why it is important to be fair and to avoid being unfair. I will discuss the first issue here and leave the second for the chapters to follow.

Social Practices

The case of the umpire who changes his interpretation of the strike zone each inning illustrates nicely why fairness should be understood in terms of fidelity to social practice. I have said that such behavior is unfair and not just wrong or tacky, and hence generically unfair. This is admittedly a disputatious claim, but I want to see if it can be made good.

We have already dismissed two ways to explain the unfairness of the umpire's actions. They are not unfair, for example, because they afford one side a comparative disadvantage. They might actually do so, of course. One team could be better at adjusting to the umpire's whimsy than the other, and this would give them a comparative advantage. But they do not necessarily lead to such an advantage; perhaps the two teams are about equal in their ability to adjust to the umpire's inexplicable shifts. The question of fairness, however, does not hang on this. We still would not think the umpire was being fair even if the two teams were equal in their ability to adjust to his changes.

Nor can we say that the umpire is being unfair because he is not following the rules. For he might be trying to follow the rule that defines the strike zone as best he can. He may think that the change made each inning brings his strike zone closer to the ideal description given by the rules. He may even think that each inning's change is actually mandated by the need to adhere to the rules of the game because it more closely approximates what the rules require. Yet even if this was true, I doubt that it would lead us to reverse our judgment about the unfairness of the umpire's actions.

Perhaps the unfairness on display here can be explained by noting that the umpire's actions affect or influence the outcome of the game and this is wrong. Outcomes, it may be argued, should be decided by the efforts of the players and not by the intrusions of officials. While the spirit behind this point seems correct, it is far too general to get to the heart of fairness. For one thing, it is simply naive to suppose that an umpire's actions will not have a substantial effect on a game's outcome. As we have seen, an umpire's interpretation of the strike zone may favor a particular team. Lamentable though this may be, it is an unavoidable feature of the game. Similarly, crucial "calls" at important moments can do much to determine a game's outcome. Like officials in most sporting events, umpires occasionally make mistakes in these situations; that is, they occasionally make the wrong call. Yet we do not usually claim that they have been unfair when they do so. Although we might think that a game was generically unfair if its outcome was decided by a "bad call," we would not also think the game was unfair, morally speaking, or that the umpire behaved unfairly from a moral point of view. This too is simply a part of the nature of the game.

Things are different, however, if we think the umpire deliberately made an incorrect call, or if he deliberately interprets the strike zone in order to favor one team. And the difference, as we have seen, has to do, not with comparative advantaging, but with the disruption these actions cause to the game. The purpose of play is compromised when one of the participants fails to be faithful to the point of the game. Making a mistake, or making a wrong call, is not a defection, or not necessarily a defection, from the game. Mistakes will be made; officials are not infallible. But deliberately making a wrong call demonstrates a failure to remain steadfast to the game, and this is what implicates fairness concerns.

The same point holds in the case of the umpire who changes his interpretation of the strike zone each inning. Even if he is not deliberately trying to favor one team, he is disrupting the game. And he is doing so deliberately if he is intentionally altering his interpretation of the strike zone. The game as a test of skill and the pursuit of a type of excellence is accordingly undermined. Pitchers are unable to throw the same pitches in the same location throughout the duration of the game, and consequently, hitters are unable to look for a pitcher's tendencies and to anticipate pitches based upon what the pitcher has done previously. Much of the subtlety that makes baseball the kind of game that it is, and much of the subtlety of play that makes some players superior to others, is lost because of the umpire's actions.

So, the umpire's unfairness is attributable to the distortion his actions impose upon the game. Everyone associated with the game can justifiably feel let down or even "cheated" in a general sense. The players can complain that they have been cheated because they are denied the opportunity to display their excellence as baseball players. And the spectators can also complain about being cheated because they are denied the opportunity to watch unhindered displays of excellence on the baseball field. The distortion of the game, and its consequent disruption, defeats the purpose of play and may well leave spectators and players alike with a sense of betrayal. This unfaithfulness, to the social practice in which he is a crucial participant, I want to say, constitutes the unfairness of the umpire's actions.

It is possible to formalize the sense of unfairness on display here by specifying its basic features. First, the offending umpire is engaged, with others, in a particular type of social endeavor that requires individuals to assume specific roles and responsibilities. Second, the social endeavor in question has a certain point; that is, the endeavor is purposive in nature. Moreover, it is reasonable to suppose that all parties to the endeavor understand the purpose of play, appreciate their roles, and understand their responsibilities accordingly. This might not be true, of course, and if it isn't our judgments about the fairness of one's actions might be mitigated in ways to be discussed shortly. But in general it seems reasonable to suppose that participants understand the nature of the activities in which they are engaged, and that they should do so. Third, the realization of the purpose that unites the participants of this endeavor requires their general cooperation (as understood within the context of the cooperative practice in which they are involved). Things go better, or as they are supposed to go, only when the participants are faithful to the common purpose that unites them. And finally, the umpire fails to remain faithful to the common purpose, and by deviating from the spirit of the game, he frustrates the cooperative efforts of his fellow participants and undermines the very point of playing the game.

This indicates why it makes sense to think of fairness in terms of fidelity to social practice. The reference to social practice introduces the general context in which fairness concerns arise and comprehends specific events like athletic contests and bargaining situations. Recourse to some such general yet bounded context is, of course, necessary in order to explain when and where fairness concerns arise and when and why they do not. But introducing the notion of a social practice at this point raises some obvious troubles. Social theorists are increasingly inclined to speak of social practices as the basic building blocks of social life; they provide the context that makes human action intelligible and understandable (Giddens, 1979: pp. 53-88; Taylor, 1985: pp. 22-37; Bourdieu, 1990: pp. 80-97; Schatzki, 1996: ch. 4). Social practices, for example, are generally understood to be cooperative ventures; that is, they are activities that people do with others (Oakeshott, 1975: pp. 56-57). As such, they are rule-governed events that are intelligible to those who engage in them.[1] They are also active in nature, which explains why the word "practice" is a proper designator for them. They are things we *do*, and things we do with others. They are the seat of meaningful (inter-)action.

From the standpoint of a philosophically informed social theory, it is possible to speak of human actions, and to separate them from, say, reflex responses, because they are embedded in social practices (Schatzki, 1996: pp. 52-73). This makes the notion of a social practice exceptionally comprehensive; anything we can do, where doing implies intelligibility, is situated in a social practice.

But there is also a tighter and more exclusive sense of social practice that emphasizes a particular way of doing. We speak, for example, about the practice of medicine or of law. Practitioners of these professions engage in particular types of activities distinguishable from the broader category of intelligible action. The distinction, moreover, rests predominantly upon the purposive, and not the active, dimension of these practices. The practice of medicine is devoted, for example, to the pursuit of good health, and the practice of law is concerned, in general, with the pursuit of justice and the defense of individual rights. The ways of doing appropriate to the practice are, in turn, fixed by shared beliefs about how best to achieve or fulfill the purpose that inspires the practice (Cf. MacIntyre, 1981: p. 175). Like all practices, these too are rule-governed, but in practices such as these, the rules put into effect and (ideally) promote the end or telos that is the point of the practice itself.

When I speak of fairness as fidelity to social practice, it is this second, more specific, sense of social practice that I have in mind. It comprehends the notions of intelligible action, rule structure, and shared activity associated with the sense of social practice at home in social theory, but it adds to this list the sense of purposiveness and action specificity (i.e., the ways of doing believed appropriate to the realization of some desired end, goal, or ideal) that accounts for the existence and operation of the practice.

Perhaps all, or at least a great many, social practices have a purposive dimension, or what Schatzki calls a "teleoaffective structure" (Schatzki, 1996: p. 101). This would certainly be the case if meaningfulness is understood to imply purposiveness, or if participation in a social practice sets the aim or direction and focus of action undertaken within the practice. Many of the things a human being can do within the context of a practice can be done either well or poorly, and if doing something well establishes a standard of excellence, then participation in such a practice can be understood to be purposive. The point of participating is to do well what the practice enables one to do (MacIntyre, 1981: pp. 175-76).

There is no point in denying that social practices can be purposive in this enlarged sense. But the more specific practices that house fairness concerns are purposive in a slightly different sense. A person can practice law well on her own and she can pursue the ideals of justice in the process. But the realization of the ends of justice depend upon the commitment of all parties to the practice. That is, practices of this sort are doubly social. They are social in the way all social practices are, viz., they involve the structured relations and associations of several, and perhaps a great many, persons. But they are also social in the sense that their participants depend upon one another for the realization of the telos associated with the practice. Fellow practitioners are, so to speak, fellow cooperators. A single individual's defection may not defeat the ability of others to realize the telos of their shared practice, but more general defection will surely do so. In short, participants in purposive practices are more mutually dependent than are participants in more general social practices.

The Fundamentals of Fairness

Perhaps, however, our umpire really is trying to be faithful to the telos of the game; perhaps he is adjusting his strike zone each inning in order to bring it closer to the proper zone and therefore to be more faithful to the game. Under these circumstances, he has not defected from the game, or at least he has not done so deliberately. Should we think, then, that his actions are still unfair?

We may conclude, under these circumstances, that the umpire is not being deliberately unfair; he is not disregarding the demands of the game for selfish or personal reasons. But he is being unfair nonetheless, and I think we can say that he is still blameworthy. The unfairness in evidence here still results from the distortion the umpire's actions cause in the game. He can, it seems reasonable to suppose, anticipate this distortion and the resulting disruption. If he has any sense or understanding of the game, he should know how his actions will affect the course of play. And he ought, therefore, to understand that consistency in one's calls is important if the game is to go as it ideally should. It is reasonable to anticipate that participants in social practices understand the nature of the practices in which they are involved and are committed to conducting themselves in a manner consistent with this understanding.[2]

Yet if it seems proper to conclude that the umpire is being unfair, we should not conclude also that he is not being fairminded, or that his unfairness is an indication of a character blemish. He might well understand the demands of fairness and be committed to doing his job as fairly as possible. And perhaps his only failing is that he does not understand properly the demands placed upon him as an umpire responsible for calling balls and strikes. While he is still blameworthy for not developing a stronger understanding of his role within the practice, while this oversight remains a betrayal of sorts, he is not deliberately abandoning the telos of the practice for personal or selfish reasons. In this sense, his actions seem less offensive than do those of an umpire who bets heavily on one team and then calls the game so as to deliberately increase its chances of winning.

This distinction is of some importance. Fairness concerns are frequently, if not invariably, the most pronounced when they arise in what I have called contested social practices. Recall that in such practices, the participants will have personal interests that can, and likely will, stand in opposition to one another and that may well matter a great deal to them. They may explain why the participants have joined a particular practice, and they provide them with reasons for defecting from the practice, but not quitting, if they think they can do so and still fulfill their personal goals.

As we have seen, competitions like sporting events provide obvious examples of contested social practices. And as we have also seen, it is a mistake to understand such practices purely in terms of interests in conflict. But it is worth dwelling on this point a bit further. In a somewhat awkward attempt to emphasize the glory of victory on the gridiron, the legendary Vince Lombardi, football coach of the Green Bay

Packers during their heyday of the 1960s, is said to have exclaimed, "winning isn't everything; it's the only thing." No doubt Lombardi's sentiment is shared by most people who participate in sporting events either for monetary gain or personal glory, but it also stands in need of qualification.

Competitors in sporting events have interests in opposition; presumably, they all want to win. In fact, this might be the sole reason they play the game. It follows, given the nature of competition, that competitors want to advance their interests at the expense of the interests of others. But they ought not do so any way they choose, and Lombardi, in spite of his protestations and along with most all other serious competitors, understood this well. For competitors must not only adhere to the rules of play; they must also adhere to the spirit of *fair* play.

Participants in contested practices, then, have divided concerns. On the one hand, they have a personal interest in winning the competition, promoting their own well-being, and/or reaping the rewards available. But as fellow cooperators in a social practice, they must also accept and adhere to the purpose and ideals of the practice, even though this will almost surely mean putting aside their personal interests on occasion.

If these concerns pull in opposite directions, as they so frequently do, it is not difficult to see which has the greatest command upon our attention. If winning matters, there is an incentive to cheat, but if participants cheat, there is no reason to play the game. Winning is the only thing that counts only if everyone plays fairly. Lombardi may have been on to something in the case of modern warfare, but not when it comes to sporting events. Too great an emphasis upon winning obscures the fact that sporting events are first and foremost cooperative endeavors where fellow participants dedicate themselves to a common enterprise.

Athletic contests, this is to say, create competitiveness within the larger context of cooperation. A bar-room brawl is not a cooperative endeavor; it is a no-holds-barred affair. Under these circumstances, it makes no sense to accuse one of the brawlers of not fighting fairly. But a boxing match governed by the Marquis of Queensbury rules *is* a cooperative activity. The contestants are bonded to one another by the fact that they participate in a particular type of purposive practice, viz., one that has an element of contestation about it. The practice, however, has a telos beyond the interests the combatants have in winning; it is intended to test their pugilistic skills, a test that is possible only if the contestants participate fairly. Winning displays a type of excellence in which the victor can take pride and which others, who happen to value excellence of this sort, can admire. But the pride and admiration associated with athletic success--dependent as it is on valuing the skills a given sport tests--depends upon a prior commitment to the game as a cooperative endeavor. We do not admire participants who cheat, even if they manage to get away with it and win the competition, and we would think them sorry characters if they took much pride in their "victory" given the way it was achieved.

Cheating is unfair, then, because it involves a particular type of defection from a contested practice. Not all defections qualify as unfair, of course. In general, a participant can quit the practice, retire from the competition, or default to her opponent without being unfair. This might irritate or anger others participating in the practice, perhaps because their victory is cheapened by the defection. But quitting is not ordinarily considered unfair the way cheating is. Cheating constitutes a particular type of infidelity to the practice. It involves an attempt to distort or obstruct the outcome of the practice and to defeat its telos by encouraging a "wrong" result.

To be sure, cheating evidences bias of some sort, but we cannot locate the unfairness associated with cheating here, for as we have seen, participants can be biased in their own favor and still play fairly. But cheating is an instance of putting one's personal interests above one's responsibilities as a fellow cooperator, and this is the sort of thing that violates our sense of fairness. Conversely, a person plays or participates fairly in some purposive social practice if she remains steadfast to the telos of the practice and honors her commitments to her fellow cooperators. As we have seen, she can still pursue her personal interests and play fairly; these are not mutually exclusive concerns. But the pursuit of one's personal interests is bounded by the standards of fair play.

Moreover, this point permits us to recognize certain times when quitting or not trying are unfair. Ordinarily, someone who withdraws from a practice is not, for this reason, being unfair. In fact, quitting or refusing to participate might be the reasonable thing to do if the practice has been corrupted by large scale defections. If and when defections reach the point where the telos of the practice cannot be achieved, there is little reason to participate, or to continue participating. Where others are expecting one to participate, however, or when one has committed to participating faithfully, quitting or not trying may result in an unfairness. Consider, for example, a problem that has recently troubled the professional tennis circuit. Some highly ranked players have committed to play a tournament after receiving a guaranteed payment for their participation (thereby increasing spectator interest in the tournament). Some players fulfilled their part of the bargain by showing up but not trying to win, preferring to lose, rest up, and prepare for the next major tournament. This form of quitting, or not trying, seems unfair. These players were hardly faithful to the point of the tournament, and the organizers, spectators, and other competitors can justifiably think that things have not gone fairly under the circumstances.

Competitions like athletic contests are easily frustrated by illicit participant defection and the unique form of betrayal this involves. Fairness checks against such betrayal by requiring steadfastness to the telos of a purposive practice. It reminds us that even in contested practices we are, and should therefore consider ourselves, fellow participants in a common enterprise first and competitors second. Fairness, then, calls us to our responsibilities to specific others, to our fellow cooperators, and emphasizes our specific attachments and identifications with particular others, regardless of whatever else might separate us.

Needless to say, athletic competitions are not the only examples of contested practices. There are others, and as one would expect, they also give rise to fairness concerns. We talk, for example, about fair trials and fair elections. In both instances, our judgments about the fairness of such events gets to the question of whether things have gone according to hoyle, with whether the participants have conducted themselves as they should and the outcome is commensurate with the telos of the practice. Elections are fair, for example, if all (and only) eligible voters are allowed to vote and if the weight the votes carry is consistent with the weight they are supposed to have.

Elections are obviously contested events. Candidates want to win, and election stakes are often high. This is reason to tinker with the results, to prohibit those who want to vote but who would vote contrary to one's wishes from getting to the polls, and to find ways to allow one's own supporters to vote more than once. Yet this is ordinarily considered unfair, regardless of how important the cause or the candidate standing for election.

Although winning will matter to candidates or to supporters of a cause, elections are not chiefly about winning and losing. Instead, they are concerned with the peaceful transference of political power, the expression of a public will, or the declaration of social policy. This is why democratic societies avail themselves of elections. Candidates for the same office, like different sides of a particular cause, are opponents in the election. But they are more than this; they are also cooperators in a democratic process that presumably matters more than the declaration of winners and losers. So, once again competition is situated in a social practice that requires cooperation if its telos is to be realized. And the type of defection from the practice associated with unfairness will once again frustrate efforts to achieve the telos of the practice and thus constitute a type of betrayal.

Similarly, the trial process within systems of adversarial justice also qualifies as a contested practice by virtue of its competitive nature. A trial is fair if the competition is genuine and if both parties are permitted to tell their side of the issue, to examine evidence, and so forth. Once again, both sides want to win, and often for reasons unrelated to the pursuit of a just outcome. In a criminal proceeding, for example, the prosecutor may worry about his conviction rate, while the defendant will worry about his liberty or his pocket book. But the trial process in a criminal proceeding is dedicated to the assessment of legal guilt. The fairness of a trial is breached if either side puts its interest in winning above its commitment to the process itself; for it is only through the proper operation of the process that an assessment of legal guilt can fairly be made.

It would be a mistake, however, to suggest that fairness concerns arise only in contested social practices, or that they arise only to check participants from defecting from a practice by privileging his personal interests over his social responsibilities. Defection based upon the pursuit of personal interests may be the most familiar source of unfairness, but it is not the only possible source. Our umpire who changes the strike zone each inning, for example, need not have any personal interests at issue. And perhaps an instructor who writes exaggerated letters of recommendation, or gives students inflated grades, does so simply in order to advance the prospects of her students. The reasons why one defects from a social practice are largely irrelevant to our thoughts about the unfairness of such actions, unless of course one defects because there are compelling moral reasons to do so. It is, then, the failure to be steadfast to some purposive social practice, that constitutes the unfairness, and fairness requires this steadfastness regardless of the reasons one might have for defecting.

Fairness and Distribution

Sometimes, but not always, distributions are made by means of competitions. Prizes and awards, for example, are usually distributed in this manner (Feinberg, 1988: pp. 199-210). But questions about the fair distribution of burdens and benefits often arise outside of competitive situations, and when they do they also give rise to fairness concerns. Consider again, for example, the principle of fairness which stipulates that one ought not benefit from the cooperative efforts of others without assuming one's share of the cost required to bring about the benefit. I have indicated (in Chapter Three) that something of the spirit behind this principle can be understood in terms of adherence to social practice. I want now to see if this notion can be suitably refined to support this conclusion.

Recall that the principle of fairness seems operative in situations where persons are attached to one another in specific ways. Where the requisite attachments are missing, or where the burdens involved are irrelevant to the nature of the attachments that are present, the principle of fairness does not seem germane. Suppose, then, we consider the possibility that the attachments which trigger fairness concerns with regard to the distribution of burdens and benefits involve the common participation in a purposive social practice.

We might begin by considering how we can recognize fellow cooperators and distinguish them from unintended beneficiaries. The notion of a social practice suggests the proper response here. People qualify as participants in a social practice, i.e., as fellow cooperators, if they are doing something with others, if that is, they are participating with others in a purposive activity or event that requires the allegiance and commitment of the participants in order to go well or as it should. In a great many formal social practices, we can recognize participants, and distinguish them from non-participants, by reflecting upon the way we refer to them. Sometimes the descriptions we give people express the nature of the social practices in which they are involved; that is, our descriptions of others often characterize them as practitioners of some sort. So for example, we may describe another as a neighbor, an American, or a baseball player, and such a description identifies by means of association. It indicates something one does and with a *specific* set of others.

But too, these descriptions also indicate something of the shared purpose that identifies the practice and unites the participants. Neighbors, for example, are presumably committed to the well-being and security of their neighborhood. At the risk of sounding old-fashioned, neighbors are not simply individuals who live in close proximity, though they are this as well. They are participants in a larger social activity, viz., supporting and advancing the domestic liveability of a particular area. Similarly, baseball players and fans share a common devotion to the game and a desire to develop and display the excellence it tests.

Of course, not all descriptions we might have for others identify them as participants in a social practice. Some descriptions merely indicate commonalities without any accompanying social attachments. We might describe all the people sunning themselves on the beach, for example, as beach users, but they are not engaged in a common social practice. In a sense, they are doing something with others; they happen to be using the beach at the same time that others are doing so. But their beach use is not part of a common endeavor; they are not doing something with others in the strong sense of being unable to use the beach but for the presence of others.[3] Nor is there a commonly recognized telos that explains the purpose of the cooperative enterprise and orients the participants in their associative activities by indicating how to proceed and what to do.

Further, not all of the social practices that might give rise to fairness concerns are formally understandable in terms of a description of the participants. Ad hoc arrangements may be made, for example, that bring together a number of persons who dedicate themselves to some cooperative enterprise. Imagine, for example, that a number of disparate individuals searching for hidden treasure decide to pool their efforts and resources and work together toward a common goal. It would surely be unfair for one of the treasure seekers to abscond with all the treasure if it was found only as a result of the cooperative efforts of all the searchers. By agreeing to pool their efforts and resources, the searchers create a common enterprise and establish a social practice that gives rise to fairness concerns. But in the absence of some descriptive feature that identifies the associative attachment of a purposive social practice and sets its telos, there must be some sort of mutual agreement, some commonly recognized associative moment, that establishes, coordinates, and directs a practice, fixes its telos, and informs the understanding of its participants.

Imagine, for example, that Sam is in the habit of buying a paper when he makes his morning stop for coffee, reading it over coffee, and then leaving it at the table when he leaves. Imagine too that Ted customarily enters the coffee shop just as Sam is about to leave and has taken to reading Sam's paper once Sam has gone. Since there is no connection between Sam and Ted, it does not seem that we can complain that Ted is being unfair if he does not offer to pay Sam for the paper every other day.

Or consider a situation where two cars are driving through fog along a sparsely traveled road. Suppose the driver of the second car follows the tail lights of the first car and benefits from efforts of the first driver to navigate through the fog. There may be those who are inclined to think that the second driver is taking a free ride here and this is unfair. To be fair, the second driver should pull ahead of the first car after awhile and take the lead, allowing the other driver to benefit from his trailblazing. A hard stand on the principle of fairness might seem to require such a conclusion. But this seems more like one of those cases where the principle does not apply, or where following it yields a wrong result. The drivers, we can suppose, are unknown to one another and just happen to be using the same road at the same time. This hardly establishes them as cooperators in a purposive social practice. If the first driver is tired of fighting through the fog, he may decide to pull off the road and let the second driver take the lead. But it seems strange to think that the second driver is not driving fairly (or being fair) by benefitting from the opportunity to follow the first driver, or that he is morally blameworthy for seizing the opportunity to follow the first car without taking a turn in the lead.

Now, many purposive practices make demands upon at least some of the participants that they may want to avoid or forego. For example, being a neighbor means working with one's fellow neighbors to secure and promote the welfare of the neighborhood. This is hardly a contested practice; there is no fixed competition between neighbors, although I suppose neighbors might sometimes compete informally to have the most attractive yard, or the like. But insofar as neighbors are understood to be committed to a common project, viz., the security, beauty, and liveability of the neighborhood, the potential for free riding is present. And where some participants may profit from the cooperative efforts of fellow participants without contributing their share, fairness concerns are bound to arise. Neighbors will have personal reasons to take a free ride if they think they can get away with it. And this, of course, is the type of defection from the social practice that sparks a sense of unfairness.

It is worth noting again, however, that there must be some nexus between the telos of the practice and the demands that fairness makes upon its participants. Because neighbors are collectively committed to the security and well-being of their neighborhood, they should keep up their yards, participate in neighborhood crime watch programs, and pick up their trash, among other things. These are activities essential to the notion of neighborliness; that is, they are (or at least once were) activities associated with the practice of neighborliness. But the practice, like all such practices, has its limits. One's neighbors cannot engage in just any cooperative endeavor and expect other neighbors to fairly assume an element of the burden. Activities beyond the reach of neighborliness do not meet the required nexus; so a neighbor is hardly being unfair, say, if he refuses to help build a neighborhood softball field, even though the field might benefit the neighborhood and thereby all the neighbors.

The bounds of neighborliness, like other purposive social practices, are malleable, of course. Neighbor understandings about the shared ends of the neighborhood are subject to change and may vary from neighborhood to neighborhood. It is, then, not always easy for outsiders to know about the responsibilities of participation in some purposive social practice. Yet some social practices have generally recognized purposes that are commonly understood by most people familiar with social life in some area or region. Most Americans, for example, have a rough idea of what it means to be a good neighbor, even if this practice is in atrophy in some settings. To grow up in a community is, in a sense, to grow into it, to come to understand and appreciate the purposive social practices present there, to recognize their ends, and hence to grasp what fairness demands.

Abstracted from the context provided by the notion of a purposive social practice, the principle of fairness both obscures and misleads. It misleads by arbitrarily linking burdens incurred to benefits received, and it obscures by hiding the associative dimension of fairness concerns from plain view. It also misrepresents the character of fairness by suggesting that fairness has something to do with payment in kind or the repaying of a debt one has incurred.

We begin to get things right, however, when we recognize that it is not the receipt of a benefit without contributing to the cost that generates a concern for fairness, but the defection from some purposive social practice. Once fairness concerns are properly situated, we see them not as a form of *quid pro quo*, but as a requirement of our associative attachments. They adhere to us as part of the description of who we are, as neighbors, business colleagues, fellow competitors, Americans, and the like. They adhere to us, this is to say, by virtue of the social practices to which we belong and in which we participate. To be fair is to do one's part, to meet the expectations of one's group, to cooperate with those with whom one is attached in specific ways even though one may have an interest in defection. Conversely, to be unfair is to defect from a practice without actually quitting, and thus to betray one's fellow cooperators.

The Limits of Fairness

There are, to be sure, many social practices that do not house fairness concerns. The easy explanation for this is to say that fairness concerns arise only in purposive social practices and not in those where there is no common or shared end to which participants are presumed to be dedicated. But this explanation is both too easy and too quick. For there seem to be some purposive practices where fidelity is not readily understood in terms of fairness and infidelity is not understood in terms of unfairness. How might we explain this?

As should be evident, the concept of fairness introduces normative constraints upon human action. An assertion that X is unfair provides a reason for not doing X, just as the claim that Y is the fair thing to do provides a reason for doing Y. Normative constraints of this sort are generally relevant when there are recognizable reasons for acting otherwise. They hold us to our commitments and responsibilities, and if we stray from them, if we fail to respect the constraints they impose, we are subject to moral blame.

From a moral point of view, fairness concerns introduce a particular type of normative constraint associated with the nature of one's social attachments. Other social practices may implement different normative constraints or house other normative considerations that are commonly or conventionally regarded to be appropriate to them. Justice concerns, for example, seem to orbit around giving a person her or his just deserts. They require us to honor these deserts even if we are tempted not to do so. And consequently, they are linked to the manifold ways of deserving that arise in different social and moral contexts. Similarly, fairness concerns are linked to purposive social practices and their normative force requires us to be faithful to their telos or ideals. But fairness concerns also seem to pull the strongest where there is incentive to defect from some practice, perhaps because the practice is contested in the manner of an athletic competition.

Needless to say, however, not all social practices are purposive in the manner that elicits fairness concerns. The practice of promising, for example, plays an important role in human relations. To make a promise is to incur an obligation to fulfill the terms of the promise. And this provides assurances to the promisee that the promisor will do what he has promised to do. It is possible to take advantage of this and to fail to keep one's promise in the event one has personal reasons for doing so. While a person who fails to keep a promise, in the absence of morally justifiable reasons, has done something wrong, we do not ordinarily consider such behavior to be unfair. While promising is a cooperative practice, in a sense, it does not involve a coordinated effort and shared commitment in the pursuit of some common goal, the achievement of a common objective, or the promotion of some mutually accepted ideal. Promising simply lacks the mutuality of cooperation present in those practices that give rise to fairness concerns.

Other social practices may qualify as purposive in the requisite sense, however, and still not house fairness concerns. Although purposive, they generally seem more intimate than those practices where fairness concerns arise. Consider, for example, the case of marital infidelity. While such infidelity is clearly objectionable from a moral point of view, we do not usually think the unfaithful spouse is being unfair. Perhaps marriage is simply not a purposive social practice, but I doubt that this is true. A marriage, after all, involves a commitment by both parties to the other and hence to the union forged by the marriage. Both parties are thus presumably committed to promoting and nurturing the well-being of the union that now sets the foundation of the family. Both are to honor and obey in good times and bad, and so forth.

Marriage presumably involves a deep dedication to one's spouse that includes a strong commitment to cooperativeness and a hearty devotion that receives partial expression, but partial expression only, in terms of marital fidelity. Marriages often fall short of this ideal, but this has not altered our understanding of the practice. And there is some indication in all this why we do not customarily think of things like marital infidelity as unfair. For while it makes sense to speak of marriage as a purposive social practice, it is not properly the marriage that matters to the participants but the marital partner. One ought not, ideally speaking, be devoted to the marriage; instead, one should be devoted to the person that is the spouse. The intimacy of the marital union, or the family union more generally, is based upon a deep caring and love for the family members, and not chiefly for the well-being or effective management of the family.[4]

Where such intimacy is present, where we look through the practice to the persons with whom we are linked, the concerns of fairness seem out of place. There is betrayal associated with the type of defection displayed by marital infidelity, of course, but it is a more personal--and arguably a more hurtful--betrayal than anything we associate with unfairness. So, where persons matter more than the practice, where it is devotion to another rather than dedication to a shared purpose that accounts for the character of the practice, there is little point in insisting upon fidelity to the practice itself.

Perhaps, however, it is possible to find a place for fairness concerns in instances of marital infidelity. Imagine that A is openly unfaithful to his wife, that B, his wife, develops an interest in being unfaithful to him by having an affair with C, and that A then forbids B to see (or have anything to do with) C. This, someone might insist, is unfair, and regardless of whether A can pull off his edict. Here A makes an exception to his marital commitment and yet refuses to allow his spouse to do so as well. Anyone who persists in thinking that fairness involves a concern for equal treatment will feel justified in objecting to all this. So I will close this chapter by considering this matter one more time.

No doubt B, for her part, will want to insist that A's edict is generically unfair. For A is having things his way at her expense, and it is surely reasonable for her to protest a situation that works so thoroughly to her disadvantage. But I don't see how we can say, morally speaking, that A is being unfair, and for reasons that should now seem familiar. If the comments above are sound, we cannot say A is being unfair by having affairs of his own; that is, his infidelity does not qualify as unfair because we have reason not to think of marriage infidelity in this way. The virtues of honor and devotion hold marriage partners together, not the concerns of fairness. In fact, the intimacy of the marriage relationship seems cheapened by supposing that fairness concerns drive marriage fidelity. It is, of course, true that A is not being faithful to the practice of marriage, and if we persist in thinking that the defection from the *practice* is what matters, we should conclude that his infidelity is unfair. But A's infidelity betrays B not simply as a spouse, but also as a loved one. And my thinking is that this matters, from a moral point of view, to the degree that it swallows the more general and more distanced concerns associated with the notion of fidelity to social practice.

So, fairness is not an issue with regard to A's infidelity; fairness concerns simply do not arise under these circumstances. Why, then, do they suddenly arise when A prohibits B from engaging in the same wrong he is committing? If they do arise here, it must be because A exempts himself from an obligation to B while holding B to her obligation to him. This, we might contend, is arbitrary and illogical, and the unfairness we might intuitively sense would then be understandable in these terms. Once again, however, the appeal to consistency is out of place.

If it is wrong for B to be unfaithful to A, then it cannot be wrong for A to insist that B honor her obligation to him, regardless of what A is up to. So, A is justified in prohibiting B's infidelity. But of course, A is also wrong in being unfaithful to B, and this is not set right by permitting B to have an affair of her own. Here a commitment to marital ideals co-opts the place where we might want an appeal to consistency to go. There is no doubt that A is acting selfishly and wrongly by having affairs of his own; he evidences no particular devotion or commitment to B, at least in this regard. This may be reason for B to quit the relationship and seek a divorce, but it is not reason to defect from her commitment to A without quitting the relationship. Nor is it reason to think that A should not continue to insist that B honor her commitment *as long as she remains in the relationship* with him. For her part, B can insist that A not have affairs in the future, and if he does so anyway, she is justified in concluding that there is nothing left of the relationship to preserve. But fairness does not sanction an expansion or continuation of a wrong, particularly in social practices where fairness concerns do not arise, and a myopic sense of consistency should not incline us to conclude otherwise.

Notes

1. Their intelligibility, of course, depends upon their rule-governed nature (Cf. Winch, 1958: pp. 24-33).

2. This point also sheds light on why coaches and players seem to want referees and umpires to be consistent in their calls, as I mentioned above, and even prefer consistency to accuracy of rule interpretation--within reason, of course.

3. This point requires qualification if we expand the circumstances to include the fact that the beach is sustained, policed, and protected by, say, the state. Now beach use is made possible by the cooperative efforts of others, as are a great many other activities made either possible or enjoyable and secure thanks to civil association. By expanding our awareness of such matters, however, we merely demonstrate that even solitary beach users are still members of a polity and thus linked, in this descriptive sense, as members of a political social practice.

4. This point solidifies a claim made in a previous chapter that a mother who fails to give an equal amount of money to her two children has acted unfairly. Here too the intimacy of the relationship is what matters and not the commitment to the telos of a cooperative practice.

Chapter Six

Toward a Moral Theory of Fairness

We now have a partial account of the formal element of fairness. Thinking of fairness in terms of fidelity to social practice offers some insight into what it means to be fair an unfair. But this sheds little insight on fairness as a moral notion. In particular, we are not yet in a position to see why fairness matters from a moral point of view. To understand this, we must consider the nature of the normative force associated with fairness. Why should we be fair? And why is it wrong to be unfair? I want now to consider these questions.

Traditions of Moral Discourse

Fairness is a moral notion. This means, in effect, that fairness introduces morally significant reasons for acting in certain ways and acting contrary to these reasons makes one morally blameworthy. Fairness, I have argued, requires fidelity to the telos or ideals of those contested practices in which one participates. But how might we account for this? And how should we understand the nature of the wrong associated with being unfair? To answer these questions, we must regard fairness as a material element of the broader formal notion of moral rectitude and unfairness as a material element of moral impropriety. And this necessitates situating the notion of fairness within a reasonably comprehensive theory of morality.

A moral theory, I will suppose, is intended to present a coherent vision of the nature of morality. It must have suitable explanatory power by means of which we can understand the disparate aspects of our moral lives and work to clarify moral confusion and uncertainty. It is not the job of moral theory to invent right and wrong, but to make the morally right and the morally wrong more understandable and comprehensible. Moral theory, then, involves theorizing about the nature of our moral life. The measure of a successful theory, as Kant believed, is the extent to which it orders and explains those views and beliefs we antecedently associate with moral conviction. A moral theory is objectionable, then, if it cannot shed informative light on antecedently recognized elements of our moral sense. In turn, moral theory is informed by, and developed from, dedicated reflection on the character and workings of these elements.

There are two familiar views on the nature of morality that compete against one another in the current literature on moral thought: The morality of happiness and what I will call interactive morality. To these, I want to add a third vision of moral life, something I will call associative morality. The first two theories are alike insofar as both are monistic and reductionist. Both hold that there is a central moral value that powers all moral discourse, and both endeavor to explain the normative force of all moral notions by appeal to this central value. Their difference lies chiefly with the fact that they identify different ultimate values as the focus of moral discourse. I will argue here, however, that neither of these views can successfully shed light on the moral dimension of fairness. To get clear on this, it is necessary to take a clue from the significance of associative attachments to which the concerns of fairness call attention. This, as we shall see, takes us toward my third view of morality.

The morality of happiness is most characteristically on display in utilitarian moral theory. Utilitarianism supposes that morality is concerned chiefly with the promotion of the greatest good, and the greatest good is identified with happiness or pleasure and the avoidance of pain or suffering. Accordingly, actions that promote happiness are considered good, while actions that hinder the pursuit of happiness and/or cause pain or suffering are regarded as bad. So, if being fair promotes happiness, then fairness has an instrumental moral value, and one has a reason to be fair.

Interactive morality, on the other hand, places ultimate moral value in the independent, and abstractly considered, individual. Persons as such are presumed to be creatures of incomparable worth and should be treated with concern and respect accordingly. This valorization of the individual introduces the normative ground that underwrites the presumptive equality at the center of interactive morality. And this, of course, returns us to the moral perspective that houses the notion of Kantian fairness discussed previously. I have already said some things intended to illustrate that our general sense of fairness cannot be adequately understood in terms of the notion of Kantian fairness. While there is more to be said in this regard, it must wait until later chapters. Here I want only to consider whether the requirements of an interactive morality, the duty to treat others with the concern and respect that befits them as beings of incomparable worth, can supply the normative force behind the concept of fairness.

By the notion of an associative morality, I mean to call attention to the attachments people have to others and to those common bonds that unite persons as compatriots of some sort. These attachments carry with them their own internal morality. From this moral perspective, membership can be seen to carry certain responsibilities. These are owed to one's fellow members and do not extend beyond the group within which they arise. They are, so to speak, the responsibilities of membership and the obligations of cooperation. If membership matters in this way, then we have reason to be fair. Our membership presumably provides us with a reason to support, promote, and advance whatever purposes or ideals might adhere to the larger social union to which we belong. As a part of this larger whole, we have reason to support it as best we can, and this requires us to participate in this larger whole fairly when and where it makes sense to do so.

The Morality of Happiness

Let me begin by considering whether the promotion of happiness provides an acceptable reason for being fair. Suppose we say that the overall happiness of affected parties is increased if people play, bargain, or trade fairly, do their fair share in cooperative enterprises, and otherwise remain faithful to the telos of the purposive practices in which they participate. If this is true, we have a reason to be fair. But it doesn't appear to be true.

The morality of happiness is necessarily consequentialist. If some conduct maximizes happiness, things go well; if it does not, things go badly (Lyons, 1965: p. 176). It is, accordingly, dependent upon empirical outcomes; the good is promoted only if it happens that happiness is maximized as a matter of fact. Given this empirical dimension, it seems difficult to believe that anyone would think that being fair invariably maximizes happiness.

To reject such a claim, however, it is not necessary to show that it is evidently false; we need only show that there are no conclusive reasons why we should think it true. And this is not difficult. Suppose Brown has a large family, or a great many fans, all of whom will be very happy if he wins regardless of whether he cheats. And suppose Green, Brown's opponent, has no fans and is, in any event, rather indifferent about the contest and will be only slightly happier if he wins than if he loses. To win, let us say, Brown must cheat, but if he does, he can win. Here the maximization of happiness would recommend that Brown cheat, and since it is at least possible that such a situation could arise, there is no reason to believe that being fair will invariably maximize happiness.

We might try to defeat this objection by introducing a number of psychological claims intended to lend credibility to the general proposition that being fair maximizes overall happiness. Suppose we insist, for example, that cheating detracts from the happiness associated with victory, increases the unhappiness of the defeated regardless of whether he or she wanted to win, and so forth, and that the result is an overall decrease in happiness from what would have obtained had things gone fairly. These claims are questionable in their own right, to be sure, but even if we accept them, we still cannot save the general proposition linking fairness to happiness. It is still possible that Brown might cheat without being detected, even by Green, and win, and that the resultant aggregate of happiness could be greater than it would be if Brown didn't cheat and lost. This is the case, for example, if the overall happiness created by Brown's illicit victory proved to be greater than Brown's defeat in spite of the increased unhappiness Brown experiences because he needed to cheat to win.

So, it is possible to imagine circumstances where happiness maximization would actually require that one cheat. And it is just as possible to imagine some circumstances where we might think that the importance of realizing a particular outcome might justify cheating. (Suppose Brown is playing chess with the Devil and the fate of humanity hangs in the balance. Imagine that the Devil is distracted for a moment and Brown notices the opportunity to cheat and thereby gain a decisive advantage. Might we not think he should take it?) Yet, even under these circumstances, I doubt we would think that cheating is fair, or more modestly, not unfair.

Utilitarian concerns may on occasion override the demands of fairness, but they do not cancel them. A person who has reason to cheat has reason to play unfairly. These reasons may, again on occasion, be strong enough to outweigh the demands of fairness. They do not mean, however, that one does not also have reasons to play fairly, or that the demands of fairness are not still operative. Our obligation to play fairly is not conditional upon whether overall happiness will be maximized if we do. Nor is this obligation suspended, or rendered irrelevant, in the event there are reasons to cheat that outweigh the obligation to play fairly. Fairness simply does not work like this. It acts as a constraint against defecting from the telos or ideals of some purposive practice, and it does so independently of side considerations about happiness maximization.

We should not reject efforts to understand fairness in the terms associated with the morality of happiness too quickly, however, because there is another way to understand the connection here. Things go better in general, it may be argued, if people behave fairly in their dealings with others. Participating fairly in those social practices that implicate fairness concerns generally makes us better off, while being unfair generally makes things worse. It is, then, the general utility of being fair, and the corresponding disutility of being unfair, that explains why we should practice fairness and avoid being unfair (Broad, 1916: p. 388).

In support of this view, thinking of fairness in terms of fidelity to practice appears to move us in this direction. Fidelity to social practice enhances the likelihood that things will go well, or as they should. It evidences a commitment to some purposive social enterprise that is necessary in order to be confident that the telos of the enterprise will be realized as fully as possible. Fairness, then, makes social life go better in those situations where fairness concerns arise, and this is reason to be fair. Everyone benefits, accordingly, if fairness is generally practiced and properly valued.

Insofar as this argument captures something of the social value of fairness, it has considerable merit. But the move from the identification of this social value to the conclusion that this value provides the reason why we should be fair is highly questionable. As David Lyons has argued, emphasizing the social utility of fairness indicates something about why fairness matters in the fabric of social life. But it does not establish why one should be fair in particular circumstances (1965: p. 177). Presumably, occasions where being fair does not maximize happiness might still arise, and if one could be unfair under these circumstances without endangering the general commitment to fairness extant in society, then this is the proper course of action under the morality of happiness.

Additionally, a moral notion's normative force--the reason it obligates--is not necessarily established by the contribution it makes to the smooth operation of social life. The concerns of morality are not necessarily functional in this fashion, or at least they are not necessarily functional in quite this way. To suppose that moral matters reduce finally to issues of social utility is to ignore other forms of valuation that may well matter in their own right. The proponents of interactive morality, for example, think it important to explain moral valuation not by appeal to the putatively functional features of moral notions, but by noting that human beings are special in a morally significant sense. If we fail to recognize and appreciate this point, they insist, we miss the underlying nature and significance of our shared morality. Before we resort to functionalism, then, it seems proper to examine the nature of interactive morality.

Fairness and Interactive Morality

Some philosophers think that morality is chiefly concerned with how people treat one another. Moral rules govern the relations of human beings, requiring that each recognize the basic dignity of all and behave accordingly. The valorization of the independent person at the center of this moral theory depends upon a particular moral epistemology. Defenders of an interactive morality understand persons as autonomous beings capable of formulating and pursuing their own ends and objectives (Downie and Telfer, 1970: p. 30). Such beings they insist, and following Kant's famous lead, should be treated with respect and dignity.[1] There is room and perhaps reason to question the valorization of the person that seems to follow rather mechanically from an account of persons as autonomous, but this is hardly the place to do so. Instead, I want to consider whether the need to treat others with concern and respect requires us to be fair.

As noted above (Chapter Three), philosophers who subscribe to what I am calling an interactive morality suppose that the presumption of equality necessitates the equal treatment of all persons unless there are morally justifiable reasons for distinguishing between them. Arbitrary discriminations between people are thus considered to be unfair and should be avoided because they fail to demonstrate the proper respect due others (Wolff, 1998: p. 106). I have argued, however, that the notion of fairness does not reduce to Kantian fairness, and more generally, that the two concepts are not conterminous. As a technical term lodged within the context of a deontic moral theory, the notion of Kantian fairness is meaningful enough. But the fact that the two concepts are not conterminous, and perhaps not even related, suggests that an interactive morality cannot adequately account for all of the various dimensions of our moral lives. This suggestion will receive considerable support if it turns out that the normative force behind the notion of fairness is not understandable in terms of the need to respect others as autonomous agents.

And there is already good reason to think that this is the case. Since the notion of fairness is not reducible to Kantian fairness, and since the notion of Kantian fairness is driven by the moral requirement to treat others with concern and respect, it would appear that this moral imperative is not operative with regard to the concerns of fairness. We have already discussed an argument that pushes in this direction. Recall that the principle of fairness works in some situations but not in others. Some instances of benefitting from the cooperative efforts of others without contributing a share of the cost of the project seem unfair while others do not. If, however, benefitting without doing one's share involves a form of manipulation or exploitation, i.e., using others as means for the furtherance of one's own ends, then it is always wrong (Sullivan, 1975: pp. 326-28; Lyons, 1965: p. 177).

According to the proponents of the principle of fairness, the wrong in question can be materially specified as an unfairness. It is unfair, in the Kantian sense, to manipulate or exploit others for one's own ends, at least when it comes to the distribution of burdens and benefits. I have argued, however, that the claim, "It is always wrong to benefit from the cooperative efforts of others without doing one's share," is false. If this is right, if it is sometimes permissible to benefit from the cooperative efforts of others without assuming a share of the burden, then the notion of Kantian fairness cannot supply the normative force behind the principle of fairness. If it did, it would always be wrong to benefit without doing one's part.

This argument is applicable more generally to other fairness concerns. If using another as a means to one's own end is wrong, then why is it not wrong to exploit an opponent's weakness during athletic competitions? By working to defeat an opponent, a tennis player appears to use her opponent as a means to the realization of her ends. She privileges her own interests in winning over the similar interests of her opponent. In fact, athletic competitions in which competitors play directly against one another seem to be unavoidably exploitative and manipulative. While they are not considered wrong or immoral, or even unfair, for this reason, it looks, from a Kantian perspective, as if they should be.

Yet it remains unfair to cheat. And if we try to account for this by claiming that cheating is a form of manipulation or exploitation, or an arbitrary way of privileging one's interests at the expense of another, we must explain why *this* way of privileging one's interests at the expense of another is unfair while exploiting a weakness is fair. While the difference in our thinking about such situations is readily explained by thinking of fairness in terms of fidelity to social practice, we cannot then refer back to the moral imperative requiring that we treat others with concern and respect to demonstrate why one should be faithful to the telos or ideals of certain social practices.

From a moral point of view, the notion of treating others with concern and respect must be intelligible, i.e., it must be capable of directing action independent of social context. Consequently, it requires us to look through social practice to the treatment of persons as such. Otherwise, moral propriety would simply reduce to social custom and tradition. If privileging one's interests over the interests of another isn't necessarily exploitative, if it is permissible under the standards of some common social practice, then one could hardly object to, say, the practice of slavery in those cultures with an established tradition of slavery. But if the notion of concern and respect is independently intelligible, and if it prohibits arbitrarily privileging one's interests over the interests of others, then most athletic competitions should be considered morally objectionable. And the fact that we do not regard them so is some indication that the imperative to treat others with the concern and respect they deserve does not indicate why we should be faithful to the telos or ideals of those purposive social practices in which we participate.

To make matters worse, it does not seem that treating another as a means to one's own ends aptly characterizes the wrong commonly associated with unfairness. It is a stretch to say that someone who cheats is using, manipulating, or exploiting another in a way that offends her or his status as an autonomous agent. Cheating, for example, is different from lying in order to get someone to do what the liar wants her to do. That is manipulative. But cheating does not involve using another as a tool; instead, it involves, say, deliberately breaking the rules of play. Perhaps this matter can be clarified by stipulating that treating another in a way that is disrespectful of her autonomy need not involve only treating her as a tool (or means) for the realization of one's ends. It might also involve, as we have said, arbitrarily privileging one's interests over hers. Cheaters certainly do this, and perhaps this is enough to abridge an opponent's right to equal concern and respect.

Yet this too seems misguided. For cheating seems both a more intimate wrong and a more generalizable wrong than this allows. Cheaters wrong their fellow competitors, not specifically as persons, but as fellow competitors. A cheater does not necessarily fail to respect his opponent as a human being; in fact, it is difficult to recognize cheating as a form of disrespect in any sense. Instead, cheating seems like the betrayal of a compatriot. A cheater detracts from the competition, and by so doing, he cheats everyone associated with the competition. All one's fellow competitors, and others associated with the practice, are implicated in the wrong; they are all victims, so to speak. For cheating defeats the point of the competition and may well distort its outcome. And it seems inappropriately torturous to twist the notion of unfair play in an effort to get it to fit the normative requirements of an interactive morality.

Perhaps this point can be made clearer by recalling two examples discussed previously. Consider again the umpire who changes his interpretation of the strike zone each inning. We have reason to think this is unfair, but how can this conclusion plausibly be explained in terms of a failure to accord others the respect they deserve as persons? Consider also the instructor called upon to write a letter of recommendation for a student and who knows that similar letters written by other instructors invariably contain inflated evaluations. If the instructor inflates her letter, she acts unfairly, and for reasons that should now be clear. But has she failed to treat another with the respect one deserves as a person?

We might want to argue that writing an inflated letter is not such a bad thing. Where others have defected from the practice, where defection is so extensive that the telos of the practice is certainly compromised, one has little reason to remain steadfast. This, as I have said, is reason not to participate in the practice, but it is not reason to join in the distortion and destruction of the practice. Once again, the fact that others are cheating is not reason to go ahead and cheat too. There may, then, be morally persuasive reasons why the instructor should refuse to write letters of recommendations for students. But I cannot bring myself to conclude that there are morally persuasive reasons why an instructor should write an unfair letter, even if others are doing so. And more importantly for present purposes, I cannot see what this conclusion has to do with the moral concerns central to an interactive morality.

Fairness and Associative Morality

Probably the strongest argument against situating the concept of fairness within either a morality of happiness or an interactive morality can be made by placing it more comfortably within an alternative moral theory. Since there is reason to think that the normative force of fairness cannot be explained by appeal to either the morality of happiness or an interactive morality, we should consider this possibility. Nor is it difficult to imagine the rough contours of a moral theory that would seem to provide an appropriate home for the notion of fairness.

This brings me to the idea of an associative morality. From the standpoint of such a morality, our attachments to specific others matter; consequently, they are the foundation of certain moral responsibilities and obligations that we owe specifically to those to whom we are attached. There is nothing terribly remarkable about this insight; most people simply take for granted the moral implications of their attachments to and identifications with others. Treason is commonly regarded as a moral wrong, for example, and not just an act of political irresponsibility. And patricide is not just another form of murder; it is doubly abhorrent because it involves taking the life of one to whom the killer is attached in especially intimate and meaningful ways.

Like its theoretical competitors, associative morality derives moral valuation from a specific moral epistemology. From the vantage point that inspires an associative morality, human beings are not merely gregarious creatures; they are also distinctively sociable creatures. We have multiple attachments and identifications, some of which may be relatively trivial, but some of which are also fundamental to our sense of self. Personal identity, then, must be regarded as a variant of social identity. We understand who we are by placing ourselves in the context of others. The descriptions we use to forge a sense of self work by grouping us with specific others. I might think of myself, for example, as Irish, as an American, as the member of a particular religious faith, as a tennis player, or as a teacher. These descriptions place me within a particular group of others; I can have a sense of who I am only by being aware of my associations.

Associative morality is premised upon the belief that associational attachments frequently, though not invariably, introduce normative constraints upon conduct. Membership often carries with it responsibilities and expectations. This is particularly true if the identifications we have situate us within some purposive social practice. If we belong to such a practice, if we are fellow cooperators in this sense, we then have reason to do our part to promote the telos of the practice and to accept and follow its ideals. We owe this to those with whom we associate in the practice. For it is only by means of the dedicated efforts of the practitioners that things can go as they should. We may defect, of course, without threatening the integrity of the practice; a single free rider may be of little consequence. But this is still objectionable; it involves a betrayal of those others with whom we are attached. It involves a disregard of what we should do by virtue of who we are.

The idea of an associative morality is hardly new, of course. It, or something like it, is on display in those moral philosophers who suppose that living a good life involves honoring, say, one's responsibilities to community and practicing virtues that help sustain one's group (Ladd, 1998: pp. 5-24; Berger, 1970: pp. 339-47). In terms of philosophical pedigree, this moral theory was common enough in the ancient world and began to erode only with the emergence of the cosmopolitanism the Stoics introduced into western thought. Yet variants of it still surface from time to time in philosophical discourse, though it is decidedly less popular among philosophers than either the Kantian inspired interactive morality or the morality of happiness (Cf. MacIntyre, 1981: ch. 4).

But we need not concern ourselves with pedigree. That an associative morality is still necessary to account for certain dimensions of our moral lives should be plain. If we do not have recourse to some such moral theory, we cannot explain why we think we owe particular obligations to family members, why treason is morally objectionable, why honor and virtue remain important moral values, and so forth. I suspect too that we could not explain why we should be fair either.

No doubt fairness, like other elements of an associative morality, plays an important functional role in the operation of purposive practices. It sustains a commitment to the telos of the practice and informs us of the great importance of fulfilling our role as fellow participants satisfactorily. And insofar as fairness manages to trump the inclination of participants to put themselves first, it functions to sustain the integrity of social practices that are endangered by the very real possibility of defections. But it would be a mistake to think that the normative force of fairness is understandable in terms of its functional role in supporting the smooth operation of these practices. That fairness helps to sustain such practices is all to the good, but we should not be fair in order to sustain them (Lyons, 1965: p. 177). If this was the case, there could be no objection to defecting from a practice (but not quitting) if doing so was certain not to defeat or frustrate its smooth operation. But such defections are still unfair; they still involve a failure to fulfill one's responsibilities as a fellow cooperator, even if the practice itself is not endangered.[2]

Instead it is the logic of our attachments itself that is at the heart of the normative force of fairness. In being fair, playing fairly, or bargaining and trading fairly, we honor our responsibilities as fellow cooperators. We fulfill the roles we play within specific social contexts and do our part to support and promote the telos of the practice with which we are identified. This is what we owe to our fellow cooperators, and it is what they owe to us. Correspondingly, defections from contested social practices that are not justified by more pressing moral considerations are unfair. Defections motivated by the selfish desire to put oneself first display a morally objectionable bias. The bias is not the source of the unfairness, however; rather, it is the defection itself--the failure to honor one's responsibilities as a fellow cooperator--that is the source of the unfairness. A person may play fairly, or remain steadfast to the practice, for biased reasons. Fairness and unfairness, in short, are displayed by one's actions and not by one's motives. One can play fairly even if one isn't fairminded.

I have suggested already that unfairness is best conceived as a type of betrayal. Betrayal, however, is different from the moral exploitation--the failure to treat others with concern and respect--that is the chief moral concern of an interactive morality. If moral exploitation involves a failure to respect others as persons, betrayal raises the moral stakes by evidencing a failure to honor a common commitment one owes to fellow cooperators. This, in turn, explains why the wrong associated with something like cheating seems more intimate, and in a sense more asocial, than the wrong associated with the abuse of persons that characterizes moral wrongdoing from the standpoint of an interactive morality.

Of course not all instances of betrayal involve an unfairness. Unfairness is best conceived as a material element of betrayal. Treason involves a betrayal, for example, but treason is not also considered to involve unfairness. Treason is a type of selling out. Deceiving a spouse while having an extra-marital affair is also a type of selling out. Both are instances of betrayal, but neither are unfair. Unfairness, on the other hand, does not involve a selling out. It exemplifies a betrayal of a different sort, usually one motivated by an attempt to profit from participation in a practice by defecting from the practice but not quitting. This is not quite selling out; it is more like selling short.

In general, betrayal seems wrong because it involves a letting down. To betray others is to let down fellow participants in some social endeavor--fellow competitors, say, or fellow shipmates, fellow countrymen, or fellow members of the faith. It is not simply another form of moral exploitation. We do not betray persons as such; it is not a matter of using others for our own ends. We can only betray fellow cooperators, comrades, or others to whom we have specific attachments, and we do so not by using them as objects, but by letting them down as fellows with whom we share a common and meaningful associative attachment. If we fail to appreciate this point, we will be unable to make much of an associative morality. But because the nature of wrongs like betrayal and unfairness seem evident enough, it is also easier to understand and appreciate the significance that associative morality has for us as social beings.

If unfairness evidences a form of betrayal, we can say that fairness displays a form of steadfastness or fidelity. One who plays or competes fairly puts the spirit of competition first and plays in a way that guarantees the objective of the competition will be achieved. In athletics, this point is often expressed by saying that competitors play for the love of the game.[3] To see the game played well is its own reward. And to take the game seriously is both to want to see it played well and to want to see it played fairly. The spirit of competition thus elicits the type of fidelity that we associate with fairness--a steadfastness to the project, so to speak, or to the pursuit of excellence that the game makes possible. Fellow cooperators, imbued with a spirit of the game, thus share a devotion that binds them together by forging special bonds of sociality which, as fellow cooperators first and competitors second, they have reason to respect and accept. This too is indicative of the significance that associative morality has for us as social and sociable beings.

Fairness and Consent

The attempt to situate the notion of fairness within the context of an associational morality will not make much sense, of course, to anyone who refuses to see social life through the epistemological lenses associated with this view of morality. If we persist in seeing things from the vantage point of an interactive morality, the associative dimensions of our lives become mere contingencies with little moral importance of their own. Moreover, an interactive morality supplies its own devices for making sense of the obligations that arise from our participation in certain social practices. It could be argued, for example, that by joining some associative practice a person consents to obey its rules and remain faithful to its telos. It is not, then, the fact of fellowship that necessitates steadfastness but the fact that one has consented to be a team player, so to speak.

From the standpoint of an interactive morality, normative force follows from two independent but related sources. Because human beings are creatures of incomparable worth, we stand under something we might call a natural duty to treat them accordingly (Simmons, 1979: pp. 13-17). This "duty" arises by virtue of the valorization of the individual so central to an interactive morality and follows rather automatically from it. The notion of Kantian fairness, as a technical term at work within an interactive moral theory, involves a natural duty of this sort. And I have argued that many of the fairness concerns that arise are simply not understandable in these terms.

But autonomous moral agents are also capable of altering their moral relationships by creating new ones or terminating previously created ones. If duties are sometimes said to be natural, obligations are sometimes said to be the consequence of voluntary action and commitment (Brandt, 1965: p. 73; Ladd, 1970: p. 3). By making a promise, a person commits herself and thereby incurs an obligation to honor the promise. So, perhaps we can successfully account for the normative force of fairness by seeing the obligation to be fair as something that rides with one's consent to participate in a purposive social practice. If so, we can explain why one should be faithful to the telos of those practices in which one participates without the need of appeal to the alternative moral perspective supplied by an associative morality. But I don't think we can suitably understand the normative force of fairness as a derivative of consent.

It is true, of course, that if one voluntarily joins some associative activity, one also consents to obey the rules and procedures that govern the activity (Carr, 1990: pp. 337-38). It does not follow, however, that this exhausts the normative reasons one might have for being faithful to the nature of the activity that one joins (Cf. Greenawalt, 1987: pp. 148-49). Nor does it follow that the fact of consent necessarily introduces the most salient normative reason one might have for fidelity to a practice one has joined voluntarily. By entering a tournament, a tennis player consents to play by the rules of the game. If she cheats anyway, she violates her commitment. But she also plays unfairly, and this will surely matter more to her competitors than the fact that she has reneged on her consent to play by the rules. Nor is it possible to conflate the two wrongs on display here. Cheating is wrong because it is unfair, but it is not unfair because it involves a failure to honor one's consent to obey the rules. The wrong associated with cheating is perfectly and entirely understandable without reference to a breach of consent.

If we think cheating is wrong because it constitutes a breach of consent, unfairness would become a material element of the formal element of "breach of consent" which is itself a material element of the notion of moral wrong. But the wrong done by cheaters seems to have little to do with breach of consent or breach of contract. We do not ordinarily think this is what we are accusing a cheater of when we charge him with playing or bargaining unfairly. Cheating is unfair, and hence wrong, because it distorts and disrupts the game, because it makes the activity pointless and defeats the purpose of undertaking the enterprise for everyone. The issue of whether one has consented to play by the rules, or to play fairly, is both irrelevant and otiose here. It is irrelevant because immaterial to the concerns of fairness, and it is otiose because unnecessary. The normative force necessary, and all the normative force necessary, to establish that one should be faithful to a purposive practice is supplied by the notion of fairness.

This conclusion can be made more credible by considering a situation where someone is coerced into participating in some purposive practice. Suppose Mary's spouse, whom she happens to love deeply, is kidnapped by a gang of chess mercenaries and Mary, who has given up playing chess, is told that they will kill her husband if she does not play in the upcoming tournament. Mary, let us suppose, enters the tournament, but her decision to play is clearly coerced. Now coerced expressions of consent, it is fashionable to think, do not actually obligate; a coerced promise is no promise at all. So then, does Mary have an obligation to play fairly?

I think we must say here that Mary does have such an obligation even though it cannot be based upon her consent to play the tournament. If Mary could escape the clutches of the mercenaries, she could quit the tournament. Her participation is evidently involuntary, and she certainly has no obligation to continue playing in the event her husband manages to escape his captors. But if she stays in the tournament, even though involuntarily, she surely has an obligation to play fairly. The fact that she is coerced into the tournament is no reason to disrupt play or to disregard the responsibilities she has to the other cooperators in the event.

If Mary is told that her husband will be killed if she does not win the tournament, and if she knows she can win by cheating, she now has reason to cheat. That is, she has reason to play unfairly. Yet this does not alter the moral claim that fairness makes against her; for she also has reason to play fairly. This follows because she is a participant in a purposive social practice that can only achieve its telos if all cooperators do their share. But here Mary might reasonably conclude that her obligation to her fellow cooperators is not as strong as her duty to help her husband. This means, as we have seen, that she has overriding moral reasons why she should play unfairly. It does not mean, once again, that her coerced consent to play, coupled with the moral reason she has for winning, eliminates any obligation she might have to play fairly.

Finally, it is far from clear that all of our associative attachments are voluntary or that we voluntarily consent to all aspects of the attachments we have. We may engage in some activities without giving clear or generally recognized and understood expressions of consent. A person must live someplace and consequently she may well end up being a neighbor. We might argue that while a person will likely have to live in some neighborhood, she does not need to be neighborly unless she also *agrees* to be. Absent such an articulation of consent, it could be argued, neighbors cannot make claims on someone or insist that she participate in neighborhood crime watch programs.[4] Yet we cannot independently re-write the terms of the associative linkages we have. We encounter our associative attachments as facts of life, and we face the responsibility of living up to them. The concerns of fairness make these responsibilities both meaningful and obligatory, independent of how we might feel about them. Social roles and associative identifications, that is, carry implications for what we ought to do and how we ought to act independent of the concerns of consent. At times consent matters, of course, but these times are themselves given by, and understandable within, the nature of the social roles we occupy. At other times, consent will not matter much, but depending upon the social roles we occupy and the attachments we have, fairness may well still matter.

Notes

1. Few, if any, of Kant's followers have expressed this point with Kant's elegance or his precision:

> Beings whose existence does not depend on our will but on nature, if they are not rational beings, have only a relative worth as means and are therefore called "things"; on the other hand, rational beings are designated "persons" because their nature indicates that they are ends in themselves, i.e., things which may not be used merely as means. Such a being is thus an object of respect and, so far, restricts all [arbitrary] choice (Kant, 1969: p. 53).

2. Suppose a competitor in a tennis match realizes he has no chance of defeating his opponent and consequently decides to call out certain shots that are in. Perhaps he does so simply in order to make it seem that he was more competitive than he in fact was but is careful not to affect the outcome of the match. Such behavior, I think, still qualifies as unfair; it skews the competition and misrepresents the skill and excellence of both competitors.

3. As a personal note, I can say that after perhaps too many years of playing competitive tennis, playing well was (and remains--in spite of the limitations that age brings) the greatest joy of the game, even greater than winning. Although I'm sure many will want to dispute the point, there are those who have found that playing one's best and losing is more satisfying than playing sporadically and still blundering past an inept opponent. If one plays one's best, there is no shame in defeat, and the loser can congratulate the winner for the excellence he or she displayed and find no embarrassment or disappointment in conceding that the best player--on this day at least--won. If one loves the game--if, that is, one admires the skills it demands and the challenges it poses--one can only find pleasure in doing one's best and seeing others--whether they are one's opponent or not--do so as well. If one does one's best and wins, so much the better. Players don't play to collect trophies; they play to achieve what the trophies signify.

4. This heavy reliance upon consent motivates Nozick's libertarianism. His objections to Rawls's principle of fairness, however, do not establish the more positive point that consent is required before obligations are incurred. Nozick is right, I think, to object to the strong, uncompromising version of the principle of fairness, the version backed, as I have said, by the concept of fairness. But his objections fail to reach the weaker, but more sensible, version of the principle supported here because he fails to consider the way associative attachments matter when it comes to the concerns of fairness.

Chapter Seven

Simple Fairness

Even if we concede that the notion of fairness is best understood against the background of an associative moral theory, there is still reason to think that some fairness concerns actually invoke the notion of Kantian fairness and belong to an interactive morality. We might even want to insist that Kantian fairness is at work in some of the more morally important fairness concerns that happen to arise, and therefore that it is more basic or fundamental to our moral understanding than the notion of fairness understood in the sense of fidelity to social practice. This possibility is inspired by the altogether plausible claim that there is an important sense in which fairness is required of us, not merely because of certain social attachments we happen to have, but because we are one person among others. Fairness, that is, may on occasion require us to look through the social practices where fairness is at issue and recognize a basic moral requirement--a natural duty in effect--to treat others with concern and respect. There are several ways we might try to make sense of this, and I want now to see if there is anything to be said for this point of view.

"Being Fair To . . ."

Sometimes we speak as if fairness is a kind of duty requiring us to do certain things to or for others. We often say, for instance, "To be fair to Fred, I must say that . . . ;" or "In fairness to Sally, she did do . . ." This way of speaking is often merely hortatory. Sometimes it is intended to display a proper modesty, sometimes a willingness to share credit, and so forth. It looks like a way of giving credit where credit is due, but in a rather metaphorical sense only. It is usually not morally objectionable for a person not to acknowledge another in this way, although it might be impolite not to do so. But because it is *only* the polite thing to do, a person cannot be accused of being unfair in the Kantian sense if she does not give credit in this manner. Her oversight seems merely foul or objectionable--tacky perhaps, or in poor taste, and so we could say that she is being generically unfair if she is being unfair at all.

At other times, it seems irrelevant or unnecessary to designate the victims of one's betrayal by saying that a person has been unfair *to* them. Although we surely could do so, we do not ordinarily say that a person who bargains or plays unfairly is being unfair *to* her fellow bargainers or competitors. She is simply being unfair, and that is an end to the matter. Her actions are wrong, and therefore we can say that she wrongs those who have reason to expect that she will act more properly, i.e., fairly. But her actions are not wrong in the sense that she has violated a right held by specific others that establishes a debt she owes directly to them as such; instead, they seem wrong because they display something like a breach of faith, because she lets down her fellow cooperators. The claim, "That's unfair," seems to presume an association or identification. That is, it presumes a cooperative relationship with identifiable others; consequently, there is little point in stipulating those who are let down by such conduct. So here a claim of unfairness seems to involve an offense against others as one's fellow cooperators, but not an injustice done specifically *to* certain others, i.e., a failure to accord them that which is their due.

But there are still other times when people seem to suggest that the concerns of fairness require us to treat others with a certain concern and respect even if this means deviating from the ordinary procedures of a particular social practice. Such claims situate fairness within the context of an interactive morality and are understandable only in the terms provided by such a morality. This is not the place to question the viability or acceptability of an interactive morality as a theory of moral life, but I do want to question whether there is any room for a concept of fairness within such a morality in anything but the technical sense commonly employed by moral philosophers working within this tradition. If, as I think, there is no such room, then we will at least have reason to question the sufficiency of such a theory of morality, and if the concerns of fairness seem comprehensible only if they are understood in the terms of an associative morality, we will also have reason to think that there is something to this view of morality.

To illustrate the type of circumstance where it might make sense to insist that the concerns of fairness should be understood in terms of a duty owed to someone, consider a controversy that surrounded a university graduate scholarship committee on which I happened to serve. The committee's charge was to award scholarships to graduate students based upon criteria announced by the funding source. To be eligible for the awards, students needed to submit applications containing the required evaluation material. These involved the usual indicators of merit: Test scores, transcripts indicating the student's GPA, and two letters of recommendation from faculty familiar with the applicant's abilities.

The troubles began when it was announced that several student applications were to be considered for an award even though their application files contained only one faculty letter of recommendation. In defense of his summary decision to consider these files, the committee chairperson argued that it would be unfair *to* those applicants lacking a letter if they were not considered simply because a faculty member failed to meet her or his responsibility and submit a solicited letter. The applicants missing one letter were treated, in effect, as innocents who should not be disadvantaged unfairly because someone else had not fulfilled her or his commitments. In response, some of us argued that considering basically incomplete applications was unfair because not all applicants could then be evaluated according to the same (required) criteria. This argument makes obvious appeal to fairness; the telos of the project involved selecting the most deserving applicants according to a specific set of evaluative criteria. Defection from this objective would thus constitute an obvious unfairness.

In defense of this view, some noted that there was nothing about the process, as established by the funding source, that seemed manifestly unfair, i.e., unfaithful to the committee's responsibility to offer awards to deserving applicants. Things like transcripts, test scores, and faculty letters are the usual indicators of merit that are consulted in order to make such determinations of desert. So there seems to be a strong case for thinking that fidelity to the requirements of the review process was necessary in order to make a fair distribution of the scholarship money.

The committee chair could have responded to all this by arguing that he was invoking a deeper sense of fairness, viz., Kantian fairness, that would prohibit the committee from disadvantaging innocents under the circumstances. (For better or worse, he didn't think of this.) And because this sense of fairness is a deeper, or more basic, moral notion, it trumps the concerns of fairness when the two conflict. This returns us to the possibility that fairness requires some baseline consideration of persons as such that is non-negotiable. Persons are not to be arbitrarily or unreasonably disadvantaged and that is an end to the matter. Might such an argument justify the chairperson's decision in this instance?

Let me approach this question somewhat elliptically by considering a possible compromise position suggested by some committee members but not adopted by the committee as a whole. The suggestion was to even things up by removing one letter from those applications with the required two letters of recommendation. This raised immediate questions about which of the two letters should be removed. If we assume that one letter is stronger than the other, we should need to decide whether to remove the strong or weak one. Since we could not know whether the letter missing from applications with but one letter would be stronger or weaker than the letter that was there, we could not hope to even things up. (In any event, it seemed implausible to suppose that all applications with missing letters were missing, say, the weak letter. If a strong letter was missing from one file, and a weak letter from another, we could not hope to even things up by this strategy.)

But the practical impossibility of evening things up is hardly the most telling reason for rejecting this solution to the problem. Suppose we consider why evening things up might allow the committee to proceed fairly. It makes little sense, in this regard, to insist that things should be evened up in order to be assured that all applicants have an equal chance of winning an award. If the point of the committee's job was to see that all applicants had an equal chance of winning, it should have resorted to a lottery. If the lottery was fair, all applicants would have an equal chance of winning, and under these circumstances there would be no great need to have applicants submit any criteria for evaluation.

As should be evident, recourse to a lottery significantly alters the nature of the distributive process. A lottery is appropriate for giving prizes, but not for granting awards. So it makes little sense to say that the committee's concern was to see that applicants had an equal chance of winning. By using appropriate credentials to manage merit, it becomes evident that we are interested in identifying the most deserving applicant. This means, of course, that all applicants should receive the same careful consideration in the review process. This is the logical prerequisite for guaranteeing that all applicants receive careful consideration, something that can be achieved only by making sure that everyone is evaluated according to the same credentials.

It would, of course, be silly to question this, but is this reason to think we should work to even things up by removing a letter from those files with two letters. Suppose we consider the matter further. In the case at hand, the awarding of scholarships involves a type of competition. Applicants compete for an award by submitting credentials that presumably demonstrate their merit. These credentials are reviewed in order to see which applicants are the most meritorious, and these are declared to be the most deserving. An adequate review can be achieved only if the credentials examined are the same for all applicants. This is reason to even things up.

But the required credentials matter; they must be appropriate indicators of the merit that is awarded by the receipt of a scholarship. Imagine, for example, that some applications lacked the required test scores. The committee chairperson could not have insisted that these applications should also be considered because the test scores are an integral indicator of merit. We might even things up, and be assured that all applicants stand equal in the review process by removing the test scores from all the application files. But this too chips away at the point of the competition. The committee would then be unable to formulate a satisfactory picture of the relative merits of the competing applicants. Moreover, the competition itself is jeopardized; by the time we are finished evening things up, there would likely be no desert criteria left to consult. And these are reasons to think that evening things up is not a proper move for the committee to make. In order to have a true competition, and in order to have a clear indication of merit, we need to have more indicators of merit, not less.

To make matters worse, the desert criteria appropriate to the competition was set by the funding source. It stipulated the credentials appropriate for the determination of desert, and if the committee was to be faithful to the competition established by the funding source, it needed to conduct its review accordingly. Thus it seems unfair for the chairperson, or the committee as a whole, to alter or amend the required credentials. The nature of the competition was set by the funding source, and not by the committee. And all parties involved expected the process to proceed accordingly.

So, two conditions must be satisfied if we are to be certain that applicants for awards receive the same careful review in the evaluation process. The same credentials should be reviewed for all applicants, and the credentials reviewed should be appropriate indicators of merit for the awards to be given. But here again we encounter a kind of misplaced egalitarianism. If the second condition is scrupulously followed, as required by fidelity to social practice, the first (egalitarian) condition will be met. For the first condition identifies the criteria to be reviewed for each applicant. Therefore, applicants with incomplete files cannot be properly evaluated, and it follows that they should not be evaluated at all. If the first condition is weighted prior to the second, a true or adequate determination of desert is no longer guaranteed because we cannot be certain that all relevant indicators of merit are present for evaluation.

To put the point more generally, if we are faithful to the nature of the practice in question, we can be guaranteed that an adequate evaluation will be made of all applicants with completed applications and that all these applicants will be evaluated according to the same criteria. The telos of the project will be followed and a "right result" achieved. But incomplete applications will not be considered. Is there now a case still to be made for thinking that this is unfair to those applicants who are not considered because some instructor failed to submit a letter of recommendation?

The idea of being fair *to* somebody suggests that there is something owed to them and to fail to accord them what they are owed is a type of moral wrong or moral blemish. But what could be owed to applicants for a graduate scholarship simply because they are applicants? Perhaps we could say that all applicants are owed an open and impartial review by virtue of the fact that they are persons whose interests should be weighed and considered equally. This, it could be argued, is a demand of Kantian fairness. But if the argument so far is sound, we must reject this claim. While it is true that the applicants should be openly and impartially reviewed, this is a consequence of fidelity to the practice itself. Such a review is required by Kantian fairness because it is an understood aspect of the telos of the practice of granting awards of this sort. For reasons just rehearsed, however, this does not necessitate the consideration of incomplete applications.

It seems more promising to suppose that it is unfair to penalize applicants, in the granting of awards and prizes, by excluding them from consideration if the incompetence of others leads to their competitive disadvantage.[1] If taken seriously, such a view would be most difficult to honor in practice. Again, if taken seriously, it appears to undermine all ability to make discriminations between persons based upon merit. An applicant could argue, for example, that his letters were not as strong as those of other applicants because his referees were not fully competent to judge his abilities. More dramatically, one could contend that her grades or test scores were not the equal of others because she was set back by a poor teacher in grade school, by negligent parents, by prejudicial social circumstances, and so forth.

Nevertheless, this principle, or something like it, has a certain appeal to some supporters of an interactive morality. If we subscribe to the liberal belief that all persons should be accorded equal concern and respect, then it seems we should also think that no person should be disadvantaged in competitive situations through no fault of his or her own. We might indicate the specific character of this moral wrong by holding that it is unfair in the Kantian sense if people are disadvantaged in this manner. And this now gives some sense to the general notion that fairness is something owed to particular persons in distributive situations.

This argument, and the liberal causes it supports, will have undoubted appeal to some, yet its acceptance leads to some curious conclusions. Even if we grant this argument, I think we must still say that fairness requires fidelity to social practice. In the case at hand, this means that applications missing a letter of recommendation should not be considered. So, if we grant the claim that Kantian fairness means that people are not to be disadvantaged in competitive situations through no fault of their own, we appear to reach an impasse. According to this view, we should consider applications with one missing letter, assuming the letter is missing because of faculty nonfeasance and not applicant error. Odd as it may sound. the demands of Kantian fairness are now inconsistent with the requirements of fairness. And just what are we to make of this?

But the appearance of an impasse is illusory if we consider the matter from the standpoint of an interactive morality. From this point of view, the thing to do is to be fair in the Kantian sense--end of discussion. Since Kantian fairness goes to the heart of an interactive morality, it must override other considerations that lack its moral stature. That is, Kantian fairness cuts through all social bricolage and holds us to the requirement to treat others with the concern and respect due them. If disadvantaging innocents means failing to treat them with the respect they deserve, then the demands of fairness should be obvious.

But surely this is not the place to end discussion. For it is far from clear that ordinary moral conviction supports this conclusion. If, as I think, it is actually unfair to consider applications with missing letters, regardless of why the letters are missing (something we could probably not know in any event), then we must conclude that the formal element of fairness is pertinent here. This does not mean, of course, that the notion of Kantian fairness is either incoherent or illicit; insofar as it operates within an interactive moral theory, it has significance. But it does raise questions about our ability to explain features of our moral lives by means of an interactive morality. Since the demands of Kantian fairness are presumably and necessarily uncompromising under an interactive morality, they should trump other less stringent normative considerations, at least in the absence of weighty consequentialist reasons to think otherwise. If, as in this case, they do not seem to do so, then we can at least say that the notion of Kantian fairness does not seem to have much of a role to play at least in this aspect of ordinary moral thought.

Now these remarks may fail to satisfy. In the final analysis, we need to measure the demands of theory against our ordinary moral convictions, and the moral understanding they generate, in order to see which theory seems the most persuasive. At some point, our own moral sense must be our guide. But of course, there is room for disagreement here too; moral sense is not unaffected by moral theory. It would be helpful, then, to press the argument further in order to strengthen the case for our conclusion, and I will do so by introducing two further thoughts.

First, we should note that if Kantian fairness mandates the consideration of applications missing one letter on the grounds that competitors should not be arbitrarily disadvantaged through no fault of their own, it may also mandate consideration of applications with no letters. For it is possible that both instructors failed to supply the requested letter. Similarly, we should also have to consider applications without, say, test scores or transcripts, or both, because these are conceivably missing as a result of clerical error or oversight. Now the granting of awards through the usual procedures becomes practically impossible because of the stringent demands of Kantian fairness. It is hard to imagine that we would want to endorse a moral theory that demands this much of us.

We cannot always know whether missing credentials are the result of faculty or clerical nonfeasance or applicant error. But these considerations rarely, if ever, enter our thoughts when making competitive evaluations. Instead, we characteristically suppose that applicants are responsible for seeing that their applications are complete, and we proceed accordingly even when we know that an incomplete application may not be the applicants fault. If we are to make fair distributions based upon competitive evaluations of merit, this is what we must do. And whatever the problems with such a practice, we do not typically consider it unfair to the competitors.

Second, the notion of fairness permits us to express a particular fairness concern about the situation with missing letters of recommendation that may better describe our intuitive moral thoughts about this example. Suppose we note, as we certainly should, that instructors from whom applicants solicit letters are themselves involved in the practice of awarding graduate scholarships. If they consent to write a letter, they in effect join the practice and become a fellow cooperator, a participant in the practice. Their failure to supply a letter, without notifying the applicant who requested the thing, now qualifies as the type of betrayal associated with unfairness. The unfairness, however, is not done specifically to the disadvantaged applicants; like the types of unfairnesses discussed above, it is more general than this. For such instructor nonfeasance distorts the competition itself. It obstructs the realization of a "right result" by making it impossible for committee members to evaluate all applicants according to the required credentials and for the purpose of determining the most deserving.

But of course, such practices often need to proceed in the face of such unfairness. As I have indicated, this unfairness is not easily offset, and other participants rarely have corrective responsibilities. But the unfairness of some fellow cooperators is hardly a reason for others to behave unfairly themselves, though if the defections of some are too disruptive of the practice there may be little reason to continue. So, an applicant who is let down by instructor nonfeasance can justifiably complain that things have not gone fairly, but she cannot fault the committee members for being unfair if they refuse to consider her file on the grounds that it is incomplete.

For the applicant's complaint, and the committee members' anger, is properly directed at the instructor who failed to remain faithful to the social practice in question.

Facilitative Fairness: Simple Accommodation

Fairness concerns often arise in situations that do not appear to involve any clear associative involvement with others. Activities like queuing up, taking turns, serving those who arrive first, and so on, indicate fair ways of proceeding, but it is far from evident that they are associated in any way with a purposive social practice. Perhaps, then, these fairness concerns are not associative in character but follow from the need to show others proper concern and respect.

This possibility begins to dissipate, however, once we start to appreciate the deeply associative nature of our shared lives. Fairness mechanisms, like queuing up, taking turns, and so forth, play a crucial facilitative role in the associative process. They provide standardized procedures which allow associative strangers to engage in certain activities that they happen to do with others and that also would be jeopardized, if not completely frustrated, without some organization and structure. These activities are often competitive; those who engage in them will have reason to put themselves first and disregard the presence of others. But they are not necessarily competitive; sometimes people will want to put themselves first simply because they are in a hurry or because they are rude.

For the most part, fairness mechanisms are a matter of social convention taught by means of social custom. Through socialization, we learn when to follow them and how to apply them. We queue up to get tickets to the theater, for example, and we think it unfair if someone crowds into the queue. This is indicative of the social character of our lives. Membership in a particular community involves sharing common social life with traditions, customs, conventions, and social habits that facilitate social interaction. To be a member in this sense is to be interwoven with others in a myriad of social practices constitutive of the social life of the community.

Fairness mechanisms support the smooth operation many of the practices and activities which need coordination if they are to go well. They come into play, so to speak, when we are in danger of getting in each other's way. Such possibilities range well beyond the usual purposive social practices that bring people together as fellow cooperators. Sometimes we engage in practices and activities in the presence of others, but not specifically with them. Cooperation, under these circumstances, is not required in order to achieve a shared end. But it may be required in order for us to pursue our own independent ends or to guarantee that things can go smoothly and efficiently. And now there is reason to cooperate by adhering to the facilitative mechanisms that promote and support the necessary cooperation. Such mechanisms are themselves purposive insofar as they enable people to get along with what they are doing in the company of others. Social recognition of the purpose and need for such mechanisms is crucial to their success and continued acceptance.

As should be apparent, fairness mechanisms apply to a host of daily activities and we invoke them generally with little forethought. They come into play, for example, when we are buying tickets to the theater and encounter others doing so as well, when we use public restrooms, when we receive service at a restaurant, and so forth. Of course, we might wonder what these mechanisms have to do with fairness. What is so fair, for example, about queuing up or adhering to the maxim, "First come, first served"? And we might also wonder why one fairness mechanism is preferred to others in a particular situation. Why, for example, should waiting in line govern the fair distribution of tickets? Why not draw lots instead, or put the tickets in a pile and let those who want them fight for them?

The first question could be answered by noting the apparently egalitarian character of the fairness mechanisms discussed here and then arguing that these mechanisms assure us that certain distributive practices will proceed in a manner that respects the interests of all persons equally. But this does not seem particularly appropriate. Crowding into a line or not waiting one's turn is unfair, but we do not usually think that the culprit has failed to respect our dignity as a person or somehow besmirched our capacity for autonomy. It is the morality of civility, not the morality of personal integrity, that seems transgressed by such rudeness and often galling self-centeredness. The "butinsky" displays a certain unsociability, a failure to abide by the ways in which we proceed in order to allow for the presence of others (Cf. Lyons, 1965: p. 177).

So perhaps it is better to answer the first question by noting that fairness mechanisms facilitate the operation of certain social practices that require prioritization to proceed, perhaps because they involve making a distribution of some sort. They are, that is, mechanisms of simple accommodation. They operate, as a matter of convention, in the absence of serious desert claims which would require that they be set aside. But they may even operate in the presence of more pedestrian desert claims that are properly set aside for accommodationist reasons. Consequently, they are egalitarian only in the weak sense that they allow distributive processes to go forward in situations where no one can assert a desert claim that justifies overriding accommodationist concerns. It is, then, a concern for facilitation, and not the need to respect others as equals, that seems central to our reliance upon fairness mechanisms.

From the standpoint of an associative morality, however, such facilitation matters. The pursuit of personal ends goes better, given the presence of others, if we acknowledge the need for facilitation and adhere to appropriate fairness mechanisms. This is an integral aspect of behaving fairly as a fellow citizen or fellow member of the community. It is, so to speak, an admission of membership and a concession to the expectations of the community. Even as we go about our personal lives, we must retain the sense of being a participant in a larger social enterprise that requires our cooperation if things are to go as they should.

An equally pedestrian response also seems appropriate to our other questions. Some fairness mechanisms are preferable to others, in certain situations, simply because they provide workable and acceptable standards for accommodation. We could (and we sometimes do) distribute things like tickets to public events by means of a lottery. But this is an awkward and difficult procedure. It is simpler to distribute these things by reliance upon a queue. In this regard, the maxim, "First come, first served," does not stipulate a desert basis. It merely identifies a procedural mechanism that orders the distribution of some goods where desert claims, if any exist, are too weak to demand recognition.

Things could be otherwise; we could distribute, say, tickets to public events by means of drawing lots, by means of a contest, or simply by casting them to the winds and letting interested parties seek them out. But the mechanism of the queue works rather well, and this is the most that can be said for it.[2] From the standpoint of fairness, on the other hand, this is all that needs to be said for it. It sets the procedure, and thus constitutes the practice, by which certain desirable goods are distributed in specific situations. Like other fairness mechanisms, it serves the purpose of facilitation and since, as associative beings, we have reason to value this end, it has an important moral dimension.

Facilitative Fairness: Lotteries

There are lotteries and then there are lotteries. Some lotteries are a gamble and people risk a bit in the hopes of gaining a great deal, but the chances are rarely good. At other times, lotteries are used to break ties of some sort. But lotteries are always a matter of chance. If the chance is real, the lottery is fair; if the outcome has been influenced, or even determined in advance, the lottery is not fair.[3] Participating in a lottery means letting chance decide the outcome; this is the point behind holding a lottery. So, fidelity to such events requires allowing chance to dictate the results. I want to talk about those lotteries used to break a particular type of tie, which I will call a desert tie. For we characteristically think that fairness requires that desert ties be broken by a game of chance like a lottery.

Consider the following prosaic example. Two individuals, Bill and Beth, both have a mysterious and fatal illness that can be cured only by giving each a full dose of wonder drug X, but only one dose of X happens to exist. Let us suppose other things are equal and we have no reason to save our supply of X. Nor do we have a more important use for it other than saving persons suffering from this particular disease. Let us suppose further that we have no particularized reason to save one person rather than the other--we are not related to either and there are no utilitarian reasons that would incline us to think that, say, Bill should be saved rather than Beth.

If we accept the conditions of an interactive morality, we might say that both deserved to be saved because of the value we attach to persons as such. Since both are persons, both deserved to be saved to the same extent and we have a desert tie. If, however, we prefer to think in terms of an associative morality, we may say that both Bill and Beth are members of our community, and as such we owe it to each to save them if we can. This too yields a desert tie since we have no way to distinguish between them as community members.[4] So neither scenario permits us to say that one has a stronger moral claim on receiving X than the other.

This of course is the rub. While we have good reason to save both, we can save only one. How should we decide which one will be saved? This, or something like it, is the type of example that seems to present the strongest case for the notion of Kantian fairness. There is, as should be apparent, a felt need to decide between Bill and Beth fairly, and it would seem that the only way to account for this particular fairness concern is to suppose that fairness is something owed to persons as such and independent of any social practice that might unite them. Nevertheless, I think recourse to Kantian fairness at this point is mistaken; it is both possible and more appropriate to explain the fairness concern at issue here somewhat differently.

The obvious way to break the tie between Bill and Beth is to use a lottery of some sort, say, drawing straws. But we might justifiably wonder why this response is so obvious. Why should we worry at all about who should receive X under the circumstances? Both cannot be saved. Why quibble, then, about how to break the tie? What is wrong with arbitrarily giving X to Bill, or with assigning X by appeal to morally irrelevant reasons (e.g., Bill happens to be a redhead and we just happen to be fond of red hair)? For that matter, why bother to break the tie at all? Since both are equally deserving, why not give half of X to each? Although this would not save either, it would satisfy some egalitarian sympathies.

I suspect most people would agree that there is something unfair about breaking the tie between Bill and Beth arbitrarily. And I think there is also something unfair about giving only half of X to each, although this claim might seem more questionable. John Broome, for example, has offered a theory of fairness that might allow for both Bill and Beth to receive half of X. According to Broome, fairness is associated with honoring what he calls claims, (i.e., recognized reasons why a person should receive a particular good, treatment, etc.), and he thinks that claims need to be satisfied in proportion to their strength (1990/91: p. 95). He reasons that fairness "is concerned only with how well each person's claim is satisfied *compared with* how well other people's claims are satisfied" (p. 95, emphasis in original); or with comparative rather than absolute satisfaction. Since Bill and Beth have an identical claim to X (viz., both need X to stay alive), both should receive the same amount of X; this, according to Broome, honors their respective claims equally and thus fairly.

Now, it seems unfair to distribute X arbitrarily, or for irrelevant reasons, because doing so does not properly honor the reasons we have for giving X to Bill and Beth. Each person deserves to be saved, regardless of the moral perspective one adopts, and to allocate X whimsically and arbitrarily fails to honor these desert claims. Because both deserve to be saved, both should have an equal chance at receiving X. In the event of a desert tie, one's desert claim does not carry the day, but it does not become irrelevant either. The desert claim can be honored, when ties arise, only by guaranteeing that each claimant has the same chance of receiving the good in question as all other claimants, hence the need to have recourse to appropriate fairness mechanisms.

The outcome of a fair lottery, of course, is arbitrary, and so recourse to chance to break ties returns us to the problem of an arbitrary distribution of X. But this no longer matters because recognition of the desert tie indicates that any distribution to be made should be controlled by chance. Since there are no good reasons to distinguish between Bill and Beth, and since recourse to bad (morally irrelevant) reasons fails to honor their respective desert claims, we have no other choice. Leaving things to chance is arbitrary, to be sure, but its fairness lies in this very fact. Drawing straws under the circumstances is fair because it is clearly arbitrary, whereas simply giving X to Bill might be inspired, not by arbitrariness, but by a suppressed desire to see that Bill gets X.

Because ordinary moral reasoning provides no way to break the tie, we must break the tie in a way that does not offend the moral reasons that establish the tie. It is the fact of the tie that elicits a concern for fairness. If there was no tie, if we had moral reasons to find, say, Beth more deserving than Bill, we would simply give X to Beth without any concern for fairness.[5] Giving X to Beth, that is, would then be necessary as a matter of justice (although it could raise a question of generic unfairness because failing to do justice under the circumstances would be wrong, inappropriate, and unacceptable).

I have said that fairness concerns sometimes arise in contexts where the mechanisms of fairness are of value in order to facilitate the operation of some social practice or activity. Ties of this sort are a case in point. We can save only one person and we have no reason to think that one deserves saving more than another. Therefore, we can honor our duty to respect the lives of both Bill and Beth by leaving the question of who will live and who will die to chance. Here recourse to chance facilitates the selection process by aligning it with our moral convictions. We understand the need to settle things by having recourse to fairness mechanisms, and hence, failing to do so--breaking the tie in a different way--is unfair. It involves a defection from the conventionally understood process--the social practice, in effect--by means of which ties of this sort are to be broken. So fairness here involves fidelity to structural mechanisms that are available to break moral ties consistent with our moral convictions.

But then, why is it also unfair to divide X in half and give an equal amount to both Bill and Beth? Consider the nature of the moral dilemma posed by the example. Given our moral views, we think both individuals deserve to be saved, but we can only save one. If we give half of X to each, we save neither. We would not think this proper; nor does it involve a fair distribution of X. Instead, it merely ignores the moral practice that brings the tie into being. It forsakes the effort to save one person fairly (i.e., in a manner faithful to the way we think such ties should be broken) in favor of some arbitrary concern for equal treatment. Morally speaking, our problem is to determine which person should be saved, given that we cannot save both. Our morality requires us to treat them unequally even though they are equally deserving. And because they are equally deserving, our morality also requires us to determine the proper inequality of treatment fairly, viz., in a manner faithful to moral conditions that create the desert tie.

Broome, it should be noted, is not insensitive to problems of this sort and would perhaps think that under the circumstances X should be regarded as an indivisible good. Faced with the problems posed by the distribution of indivisible goods, Broome also argues for the use of a lottery to break desert ties. But his argument commits us to some odd sounding conclusions. These are a result of his insistence that fairness demands the satisfaction of a valid claim--something that approaches the notion of justice as I understand it. In the case of indivisible goods, valid claims cannot all be satisfied; therefore, some unfairness is bound to result. Speaking specifically about desert ties involving indivisible goods, he says,

> claims cannot all be equally satisfied, because some candidates will get the good and others will not. So some unfairness is inevitable. But a sort of partial equality in satisfaction can be achieved. Each person can be given a sort of surrogate satisfaction. By holding a lottery, each can be given an equal *chance* of getting the good. This is not a perfect fairness, but it meets the requirements of fairness to some extent (1990/91: pp. 97-98, emphasis in original).

Now, this argument seems objectionable for two reasons. First, it seems wrong to insist that some unfairness is inevitable when we face desert ties involving the distribution of an indivisible good, and second, it is also doubtful that perfect fairness is not achieved by appeal to a lottery. Perhaps perfect justice cannot be done when desert ties are present, but this is a different matter. And because perfect justice might not be possible, we might think things are generically unfair, but this is a different matter too.

Broome's argument presupposes that fairness concerns arise in distributive situations independent of, and prior to, desert ties. (This will be the case if a distributional question arises within the context of a purposive social practice, but it need not do so.) Ideal fairness, according to Broome, is achieved when all parties' claims are satisfied. Here fairness is owed to particular individuals by virtue of their claim to some good. So, things go fairly if two doses of X exist and both Bill and Beth get one. But it isn't at all clear that fairness concerns attach to the example in quite this way. Suppose Bill does not exist and Beth is not given X. Broome would not say this is unfair since he thinks fairness is fundamentally comparative; to be fair, valid claims should be honored equally. But why do things change once Bill is introduced?

Suppose Bill is back in the equation and we find another dose of X. We give one to Bill but still do not give one to Beth. This is unfair, Broome would have us say, because of the comparative advantage accorded to Bill. But the wrong done to Beth results from the fact that we did not give her a dose of X and has nothing to do with how we have treated Bill. As I have labored to show, abstract equalities are irrelevant to the concerns of fairness. (If Beth's failure to get a dose of X results from a defection from a purposive social practice that stipulates she should receive X, then it is unfair not to give her a dose of X, regardless of what happens to Bill.) Unhinged from a pertinent social practice, then, it is simply mistaken to think that the just treatment of either Bill or Beth has anything to do with fairness.

If this is right, then fairness concerns do not arise prior to the desert tie, and correspondingly, settling the tie fairly must be considered "perfectly fair." Absent the tie, we need not concern ourselves with fairness; we need only see that the parties involved receive their just deserts. It is only when it is not possible to accord both parties their just deserts that we face a problem of fairness. For we must decide how to proceed with a distribution when the circumstances don't allow us to make the kind of distribution we think we should. Appeal to appropriate fairness mechanisms allows distributors to resolve desert ties fairly, i.e., in a manner faithful to the claims that bring about the tie. If an appropriate fairness mechanism is faithfully executed in order to resolve a desert tie, the demands of fairness have been met, and met fully. That is, the tie has been broken fairly. This is hardly surrogate satisfaction; under the circumstances, this is all the satisfaction to which one is entitled. And if the distribution is faithful to the outcome of the fairness mechanism employed, it follows that the distribution is a fair one. Perhaps then we should say simply that it seems possible to be perfectly fair even in a world that does not allow us to be perfectly just.

Taking Turns and Respect For Others

The mechanisms of simple fairness are easily misconstrued. Seeing them at work may incline some to think that fairness has something to do with treating others with the respect they deserve as persons. I have argued that his is a mistake, but since the mistake is tempting, I will labor the point a bit more. Consider the little story offered by Elizabeth Cote in her primer intended to teach the virtue of fairness to children.

> The recess bell rang and everyone filed out to the playground. Brian grabbed the kickball on his way out and yelled, "Come on! Let's play! I'll be the pitcher."
>
> "You're always the pitcher, Brian. I'd like to try it,"
> protested Danny.
>
> "I got here first, so I get to be the pitcher."

> "You should let someone else pitch," said Levon. "Why don't you play the field today?"
>
> "I'd like a turn at pitching too," said Lillian. So did Debbie, Eli, and Cam.
>
> "Well, we can't all pitch," said Levon. "Since there are five who want to be pitchers, we can have one for each day of the week. Danny can pitch today" (Cote, 1989: p. 31).

Cote apparently supposes that Levon makes the best case for fairness (in spite of his authoritarian style). And we might want to explain this by insisting that Levon understood the need to respect all the participants in the game. Because everyone counts, no one should have her or his interests or desires frustrated or blocked by others, like Brian, who might want to hog the limelight.

Yet I think this misrepresents the true (if not the intended) moral of the story. Considered abstractly, it is hardly unfair to permit Brian to pitch all the time, even if others want to do so. If the game involved a competition against another team and Brian was the best pitcher, it would be reasonable to have Brian pitch, and doing so seems to be entirely fair, even if some of the children still wanted to pitch.

Why, then, is it not fair to permit Brian to go on pitching? The obvious answer is that other children want to try pitching. But why should that matter? There are, as we just observed, clear situations where it doesn't seem to matter, or at least to matter much. Perhaps we should say it matters under the circumstances because Brian is faced with a little rebellion of sorts. The game is in danger of being thrown into disarray and is consequently in need of some coordination. The need for some organizational structure, in the absence of some generally understood and accepted method of proceeding, is met by the invocation of a particular fairness mechanism.

However, this may seem like a somewhat cynical way to take the story. Recall Levon's admonition to Brian that he should let someone else pitch. Presumably, this implies that taking turns is owed to the participants and that they are being cheated, in a sense, by not receiving their just deserts. But it seems silly to think that all the children deserve a shot at pitching. They are not owed anything of the kind, and if Danny and the others did not want a turn, it seems unlikely that anyone would insist that Brian should let others pitch. So, Levon's admonition seems powered by the need to consider the fact that others want to pitch. And we can still wonder why this should matter.[6] I suggest it matters because it creates something like a desert tie. In the face of competing wants, there is no fair way for the children to proceed with the game, except to invoke a mechanism of simple fairness.

But why have recourse to taking turns? Why not draw straws or invoke first come, first served (which would again give Brian the ball)? If taking turns is the "right" mechanism to invoke, we again may have a case for Kantian fairness. Taking turns, however, seems like the right mechanism because it is really the most prudent mechanism. It guarantees that each child's want-claim (which seems recognized by the children as something like a desert basis) will be satisfied consistent with the claims of all the others. First come, first served will favor the speedy and a lottery cannot guarantee that everyone's want-claim will be honored. So, taking turns seems the prudent choice, and consequently, none of the children can have reason to object.[7]

Cote's story, then, really does reveal something of the nature of fairness, although probably not what she had in mind. It suggests the depth that fairness mechanisms seep into our daily lives and the considerable importance they have for us. They introduce ways for getting on and going along, and they make coordination possible in the absence of otherwise understood and recognized methods for proceeding. They are, that is, indispensable virtues of an associative morality.

Notes

1. In the language attributed to Barry earlier, we could say that a faculty member's failure to write the required letter created a condition of background unfairness. Of course, if this claim is sound, the committee would have to consider all incomplete applications. Its members could not know, without further investigation, whether, say, transcripts were not submitted because of clerical error or because applicants failed to request them. It is not possible to know this in the case of letters of recommendation either, of course. But if we presume faculty error in one situation, consistency would require us to presume clerical error in the other. Interestingly, the committee chair did not want to go this far, and he did not think it unfair to exclude applications with missing transcripts.

2. It is, however, efficiency and not utility that makes the queue acceptable in these circumstances. General happiness might be increased by a different distribution of tickets than the one that results from resorting to the queue. But the distribution of generally desired goods, like tickets to sporting events, is rarely controlled by the standards of utility. If utility preferences matter, they may be implicitly recognized by the cost people bear in applying fairness mechanisms. A person who really wants a ticket to the Super Bowl should get in line early, for example. But this is still no guarantee that the queue will result in a utility maximizing distribution. Those who would be happiest to receive a ticket may not be able to afford the cost imposed upon them by reliance upon the queue.
More to the point, however, we think the distribution of such public goods should be made fairly, or by recourse to the appropriate fairness mechanism, and not by making utility calculations. An unfair distribution of tickets would be objectionable even if it maximized general utility.

3. Some lotteries may draw winners from previously distributed lots; others may distribute lots after the drawing has been done but the outcome not announced. For present purposes, we need not worry about the difference. While the procedures differ, the element of chance can still be maintained in both systems.

4. If, however, Bill was a community member and Beth was not, we would have reason, under an associative morality, to give X to Bill rather than Beth. Nor is this altogether abhorrent from an intuitive viewpoint. Our responsibilities to aid others seem tied to our association with them, and this gives additional credibility to an associative morality. If Bill did not need X, there would be reason, morally speaking, to give it to Beth. But our first responsibility is to care for our own (Cf. Walzer, 1983). From a moral point of view, if membership matters in this fashion, we have further reason to take seriously the notion of an associative morality.

5. I suppose Bill might object to this by claiming that this was generically unfair, i.e., inappropriate, foul, or whatever, but such a claim could not be substantiated given the moral weights attached by the example.

6. Parents, teachers, or observing adults may think it matters because they do not want any of the children to feel left out or slighted in any way. That is, it matters from this point of view because we worry about the children's sense of self, as well as their feelings. But we can suppose this is not something that matters to the children themselves.

7. Brian, however, may have reason to object since it seems he is being left out of the pitching rotation. Counting Brian, six children, rather than five, want to pitch. Levon's calling, it seems, is to moral philosophy and not to mathematics.

Chapter Eight

Fair Procedures

A good deal has already been said about the fairness of rules and procedures. They are fair if faithful to the telos of the practice they regulate, govern, guide, or constitute. But perhaps this does not go far enough. Fair procedures, it may be argued, should promote, reflect, and support the need to show persons equal concern and respect. According to this view, the procedural methods by which agreements are reached and resources are distributed should be governed by the requirements of Kantian fairness and should aim at fair outcomes, often knowable independent of procedure. This introduces the last possible way to defend the notion of Kantian fairness that I want to consider.

Hard Bargains

To begin, let me return to the subject of bargaining. It has been argued that a bargain is fair if the bargainers reach a mutually acceptable equilibrium point by bargaining in an honest, forthright, and dedicated manner. Bargainers remain free to pursue their own interests within the context of fair bargaining, but a bargaining situation is not a war--bargainers cannot fairly do just anything in the pursuit of a favorable outcome. And regardless of outcome, a bargain is fair if it is fairly bargained. While some range of acceptable equilibrium points must be presumed by bargainers if they are to proceed, there is no specific "right result" toward which the bargainers should work.

As we have seen, this last point is controversial. Recall, for example, Raphael's claim that a bargain reaches a right result only if the bargainers are equally advantaged (or almost equally advantaged) by the outcome (Raphael, 1955: p. 54). Nor is Raphael alone in thinking that bargains have antecedently fixed results that should be reached, or at least approximated, through the bargaining process. Michael Sandel, for example, claims that "contracts bind not because they are willingly incurred but because (or in so far as) they tend to produce results that are fair" (1982: p. 107). As Sandel correctly notes, this makes sense only if there is some independent criterion of fairness that determines the proper outcome of a contract or (presumably) more general bargaining situation. This implies, in turn, that there is some independent moral need for bargainers to respect one another as equals. And this returns us to Kantian fairness.

But it seems that all this concern for outcomes fails to take the nature of bargaining seriously enough. Bargaining involves a process; or rather, bargaining *is* a process. The outcome of this process, the agreement reached or the "meeting of the minds" at issue in contract law, determines the responsibilities and expectations of the bargainers. If a "fair" outcome was knowable in advance, there would be little reason to engage in the process. We can speak of an outcome as fair, however, only because of our legitimate concerns for the fairness of the process, or of the way the outcome was reached. In a bargaining arrangement, like an athletic competition, personal goals are pursued within a broader context of cooperation, and cooperators, to be fair, must adhere to the appropriate procedures.

An agreement reached as a consequence of unfair bargaining must result in an unfair outcome, even if the parties involved are reasonably happy with the result. We cannot know if the parties would have reached the same agreement had things been bargained fairly, but this doesn't matter in any event. For when it comes to bargaining, it is not a matter of getting to the right outcome, but a matter of getting to an outcome fairly. Ordinarily, if we see an outcome that seems to favor one of the bargainers, we might think that something unfair has happened. Or, if we see an outcome that equally advantages all bargainers, we might think things have gone fairly. But such conclusions are unwarranted, because it is the process that matters. If we discover that an outcome which appears to wildly favor one bargainer and disfavor another was reached by means of open, honest, and forthright bargaining, with both parties fully able to look out for their own interests, we must concede that the bargain, including the outcome, is fair.

Consider, however, what I will call "hard bargaining" situations. Hard bargains are struck when one of the bargainers is in position to take advantage of the other. Imagine, for example, buying chains in a snow storm or purchasing Super Bowl tickets from a scalper. An even more salient example is presented by Nozick in order to illustrate what he calls coercive offers (Nozick, 1969: pp. 440-72; Cf. Haksar, 1976: pp. 65-79; Held, 1978: pp. 49-62). Nozick supposes that someone, say Pat, is drowning and Paul happens to be passing by in a boat and recognizes Pat as a millionaire in distress. Paul offers to save Pat for the handsome sum of one million dollars. Suppose Pat happily consents to the offer (it sounds like a good deal at the time) and Paul hauls her out of the water. Upon reaching shore, a grateful Pat pays off; end of story. Has anything unfair happened?

Paul has admittedly taken advantage of Pat's predicament to benefit himself wildly, but Pat, for her part, has little grounds for complaint. She may also consider herself wildly better off thanks to her deal with Paul than she would otherwise have been. From her viewpoint, the deal may have been well worth it; in fact, she may have been willing to pay a good deal more for Paul's help. It is difficult to say, then, that Raphael's requirement of roughly equal advantaging has not been met. More importantly, however, it also looks as if a suitable equilibrium point was reached by two independent bargainers. Consequently, we have some reason to conclude that the deal reached was fair.

Still, this is a troubling conclusion; it seems more intuitively appealing to claim that there is nothing fair about any of this. We might want to explain this by holding that Paul exploited Pat's unhappy condition for his own advantage, and according to the strictures of Kantian fairness this is unfair. This entitles us to say that the deal really was unfair in the Kantian sense because Paul's treatment of Pat was unfair. But we need not resort to the notion of Kantian fairness at this point to avoid the conclusion that Paul's actions were not fair. They are neither fair nor unfair, for instance, if fairness concerns simply do not arise under these circumstances. And I think this is the proper conclusion to reach. If this is right, then the notion of fairness does not get to the type of moral blame we should ascribe to Paul, and we should avoid a theoretical account of fairness that would require us to think that it does.

Paul obviously had the means and ability necessary to help Pat. From a moral point of view, it makes some sense to insist that he also had good reasons, even the duty, to do so. That is, we can suppose that all the moral perspectives introduced above supply reasons why a person should aid or rescue persons in distress if they can do so without great risk. The utilitarian case is reasonably straightforward; rescue is likely to increase overall happiness since Pat's joy at being rescued will surely exceed whatever cost Paul suffers in performing the rescue. From the standpoint of an interactive morality, things are also straightforward. Valuing persons as beings of incomparable worth entails a duty to come to the aid of those in need.

The moral requirement to rescue is uncertain only in the case of an associative morality (although it can be made uncertain in the case of utilitarianism). If we assume that the individuals involved are linked together as fellow cooperators of some sort, and if the conditions of cooperation involve mutual aid, as they surely do, for example, if Paul and Pat are fellow citizens in a common polity, then an obligation to rescue follows unproblematically. If there are no such associative attachments, however, no obligation to rescue follows from an associative morality, although human empathy may incline someone to want to rescue another in such need. In fact, both associative and utilitarian perspectives might tolerate or even require issuing a coercive offer under some circumstances.. (Imagine Pat is an enemy soldier during wartime and Paul has reason to think Pat knows many important military secrets. Paul tells Pat he will rescue her only if she reveals those secrets. Or imagine Paul is visiting a culture that practices a form of human sacrifice and Pat has been chosen as the sacrificial victim.) I will suppose, however, that the example is contextualized in such a way that all three moral perspectives provide Paul with reasons for rescuing Pat.

If it is reasonable to suppose Paul was morally obligated to rescue Pat, then morally speaking there was nothing for him to bargain about. It makes no sense to conclude the bargain was a fair one, then, because this was not a bargainable issue. From a moral point of view, Paul was not free to negotiate Pat's rescue. His obligation to aid a person or fellow in distress precluded any negotiation on the subject. Consequently, there is no proper *quid pro quo* imaginable under the circumstances. We could not say, for example, that the deal was unfair if Paul agreed to rescue Pat for one dollar on the grounds that this hardly compensated Paul for his efforts. Under the circumstances, his efforts are owed to the person or fellow in distress. And Paul's offer to rescue qualifies as coercive for just this reason; Pat should not have to face Paul's attempt to leverage her to his advantage at this particular moment (Carr, 1988: pp. 59-68).[1]

It seems, then, that Paul's actions are neither fair nor unfair; fairness concerns simply do not arise in coercive situations. Recourse to the notion of Kantian fairness, however, counsels otherwise. From the standpoint of Kantian fairness, it looks as if Paul acted unfairly and the bargain struck was an unfair one. If this fails to accord with our intuitive belief that fairness concerns really do not arise under the circumstances, we have another reason to reject efforts to place the notion of fairness within the context of an interactive morality.

It would be a mistake to conclude, however, that hard bargains always or necessarily involve properly non-bargainable situations. The opportunism associated with hard bargaining is relatively common. When it rains, the price of umbrellas goes up; when it snows, the price of snow tires rises. And sometimes this is altogether fair. Sometimes prices go up simply because demand goes up and reasonable market adjustments are to be expected. And changes in circumstances, like shifts in the weather, can do much to alter demand. At other times vendors may raise their prices because they think consumers will continue to buy even if there are no great changes in circumstances that may affect the market. If they don't, prices will decline again; such is the nature of the market.

Excessive opportunism, however, is generally frowned upon. Courts of law, for example, occasionally nullify contracts as unconscionable if one party took advantage of the circumstances of another to provide a service for a fee considerably in excess of the standard market value of the service. And this seems appropriate; for there does seem to be something unfair about this sort of opportunism. But we need not make appeal to the notion of Kantian fairness to understand this. Excessive deviation from market value for opportunistic reasons is itself a defection from a purposive social practice. Participants in a market transaction are fellow cooperators in a practice that allows the exchange of goods and services for mutually advantageous purposes. Like bargainers, these participants seek to promote the interests of each by identifying an acceptable equilibrium point. The market indicates a standardized equilibrium arrived at as a result of balancing the respective interests of all transactional participants. So, defection from the market when a fellow participant is under external conditions of duress is a way to put oneself first by deviating from the standards that control the associative arrangement in question. It is hardly faithful to the spirit of the market as a means for promoting mutual advantage. It is a form of cheating, and as such, it is unfair.

Still, markets do allow changes in circumstances to influence anticipated equilibrium points. As needs change, perhaps as a result of changing external circumstances, the value of commodities changes as well and the market understandably reflects this. Umbrellas are more valuable in winter and a towing service may cost more in a snow storm. This is a feature of market practice and is largely understood to be faithful to the spirit of market exchanges. So, any clear line between fair hard bargains and defections from market practices is difficult, if not impossible, to draw with precision. The line depends, in the end, on our understanding of the market practices and the generally understood sense of proper and improper dealing associated with it.

Fairness and Rational Choice

There is another way to support the idea that fair agreements have antecedently determinable outcomes as required by Kantian fairness. Consider a situation common to rational choice theory. Imagine that two people, one (W) very wealthy and the other (P) quite poor, are asked to reach an agreement on how to share $200. Before the money can be distributed, they must agree to the terms of the division; thus each party can veto any distributive proposal. If no agreement is reached, the money is not distributed. Raphael, and perhaps Sandel, would likely say that a fair outcome would give both W and P $100 each. Of course, we might not think this very just if P is more needy than W and if we think need operates as a viable desert basis in this situation. This, however, is to be concerned with justice and not with fairness.

But suppose W insists on receiving $150 knowing that the relative marginal utilities favor her and that P is better off settling for a mere $50 than going without altogether. Since W has no problem with going without, she is in the strongest bargaining position and can set the terms of the deal (Raiffa, 1982: p. 52). Imagine, then, that P settles for $50, leaving the rest to W. Is this deal fair? Should we say here that the deal is fair but that the outcome is unfair in the Kantian sense?

One way to argue against this conclusion is to claim that suitable conditions of background fairness are not realized under the circumstances. But the notion of background fairness is suspicious in its own right, as we have seen; so there is reason to avoid this move. We can, however, question whether W bargains fairly when she brings the realities of marginal utility into play. Recall that the bargaining process involves an effort by the parties to the bargain to hit upon an agreement that acceptably promotes the interests of each. To participate in the social practice of bargaining is to search for the proper equilibrium point at which the respective interests and concerns of the parties involved are maximally realized and respected. One violates the spirit of the bargaining process if one looks for ways to leverage one's fellow bargainers in order to promote one's own interests at their expense. That is, one bargains unfairly if one attempts to impose an agreement upon one's fellow bargainers instead of working toward a mutually acceptable agreement.

In some bargaining situations, there is arguably not much to bargain about. If W and P need to find a mutually acceptable way to split $200, concern for a mutually beneficial agreement would appear to recommend an equilibrium where each takes $100. Yet if things were this straightforward, there would be no point to the bargaining; there would be no reason for bargaining in order to distribute the money. The proper outcome would be evident independent of any bargaining arrangement. But as I suggested in Chapter Four, the bargaining process does seem to matter because equilibrium must be reached; it cannot simply be found. As we have seen, it would be unfaithful to the telos of the bargaining process for W to leverage P by threatening not to reach an agreement unless W gets the greater share of the money; for W is not now working toward a mutually acceptable agreement. It does not follow, however, that a mutually acceptable agreement must be based upon considerations of simple equality.

Perhaps W will be moved by P's plea of need; perhaps, in fact, W will be willing to settle for an amount considerably less than $100. Let us suppose, then, that P makes a case for an equilibrium that would bring him $150 and leave $50 for W. This approximates the outcome favored by at least some considerations of justice since P is quite needy and W is well-off. If W accepts on the grounds that her interests are satisfactorily met and P's interests are properly advanced, the bargain would seem to be fair. But similarly, if W objects and indicates that she favors dividing the money into equal shares, and if P accepts this proposal because it looks like the best possible deal under the circumstances, the concerns of fairness are again satisfied. Here P has no grounds for complaint because the interests of both parties have been maximally satisfied, even though his particular interests have not been.

It may be objected, however, that the first scenario, where W settles for $50 and leaves $150 for P, is actually unfair since W does not seek to maximize her own interests. Here neither P nor W are in search of an arrangement that would maximally advance the interests of each. We need not worry about this, however, if we suppose that both W and P recognize that the obvious equilibrium point is to split the money equally. Assuming both want as much money as possible, this outcome satisfies the maximum mutual advantage condition. But we need not suppose that fairness requires the bargaining process to end there. Unlike the rational choice scenario, P is not trying to leverage W into making a deal worse than what is required by mutual advantaging. Instead, P is asking W to consider his situation to see if perhaps she might not want to settle for a lesser amount and permit him to enjoy a much needed benefit. If W is unwilling, that is an end to the matter; if W is agreeable, the matter reaches a different end.

This is certainly permissible under an associative morality (where there is reason to care about the well-being of one's fellows) and the morality of happiness (where happiness will be maximized). And it seems strange to think the bargain is unfair if

W accepts the lesser amount of money because mutually beneficial results were not forthcoming. If W is happy with the deal, even though she could have gotten more and she knows this, and if the deal has been the result of fair dealing (i.e., no deceit, leveraging, intimidation, and so forth), then the outcome is surely fair. And it would be fair even if W permitted P to have all the money. It is, once again, the fairness of the bargaining that makes a bargain fair, and not its outcome.

Perfect and Imperfect Procedural Justice

Perhaps we can say, then, that procedure determines the fairness of a distributive outcome in at least some situations. But must it do so in all such situations? John Rawls, for one, does not think so. His familiar distinction between pure procedural justice and perfect or imperfect procedural justice is intended to separate those situations where procedure is essential to the determination of a fair outcome from those where it is not.

Situations where procedure is determinative of the fairness of an outcome are, according to Rawls, matters of pure procedural justice. But in cases of perfect and imperfect procedural justice, he thinks the fairness of an outcome can be known independently of procedure. In the case of perfect procedural justice, he supposes that fairness can be known prior to the outcome of process and that procedures can be devised that guarantee the fair outcome will be realized. Presumably, the purpose behind devising such procedures is to be certain that the antecedently understood fair outcome is realized. In the case of imperfect procedural justice, on the other hand, Rawls again supposes that the desired outcome can be known in principle (though not in fact), but he also thinks that it is not possible to establish procedures that will guarantee the desired outcome (1971: p. 85). Procedures should enable us to push in this direction, but they cannot guarantee what we understand in principle to be a fair outcome.

Rawls illustrates the notion of perfect procedural justice by appeal to a simple case involving two individuals dividing a cake between them. He assumes, in a fashion reminiscent of Raphael, that a fair division is an equal division (1971: p. 85). A fair procedure can now be devised that guarantees this outcome, viz., one person cuts the cake and the other selects which piece he will take.

Needless to say, this situation presumes the simple egalitarianism that underlies the notion of Kantian fairness. It supposes that respecting persons as equals here necessitates an equal distribution of the cake. Presumably, the distribution should be equal because neither party has a prior or more compelling claim on the cake, therefore, the interests of the two parties are equally represented simply by allocating half the cake to each. The problems with this view, however, have been anticipated already. The cake example is similar to the rational choice problem considered above. If we suppose that a fair distribution is an equal distribution, then a procedural mechanism can be devised that defeats the ability of one party to play with marginal utilities to his advantage. So, procedures can guarantee a right result.

But we might wonder why we are justified in thinking at the outset that an equal distribution is a fair distribution. We might want to say here that each party's interest in getting "his share" should be respected in the absence of any recognizable desert claim. And the need to show equal respect for each party's interests presumably follows from a sense of Kantian fairness. Since we also presume that each party wants as much of the cake as possible, and would gladly take it all if circumstances allowed, an equal division constitutes a fair division.

Let me dwell on this view of the matter for a moment. It does not appear that desert considerations are completely absent from this situation. The requirement to treat persons with equal concern leads to the conclusion that the interests of each party deserve to be considered in the distributive process. This desert claim might even be said to follow from the more basic desert claim which stipulates that each person deserves equal concern. This is the fundamental nature of Kantian fairness, or as I prefer to say, justice. But how do we get from this point to the conclusion that each party should receive half the cake in order to arrive at a fair outcome?

We could invoke the standards of simple fairness at this point. The respective interests of the two individuals in getting as much cake as possible creates a desert tie. We need to respect these interests and we need to do so equally in the absence of other relevant desert considerations. So, perhaps we can use a fairness mechanism to break the tie. But which one? Why not treat the cake as an indivisible good, or as a good whose value is defeated by making a division, and simply flip a coin or draw lots? Why would this not yield a fair outcome? Would it fail to do so if the parties involved preferred flipping a coin and playing all-or-nothing to cutting the cake in half?

Perhaps we can avoid this indeterminate situation, if one really wants to avoid it, by arguing that respect for each person's interests establishes (for some reason) that each person deserves half the cake. Now honoring the respective desert claims requires an equal distribution of the cake. I doubt this argument can succeed because I don't see how we can get to the conclusion that each person deserves half (or an equal share) of the cake from the more general moral claim that each person deserves to have her or his interests respected in the distributive process. At best, this establishes a desert tie that might be broken by appeal to several fairness mechanisms, rather than a desert claim against half (or an equal share) of the cake.

But even if we tolerate this move, the argument still does not do much to indicate why an equal distribution is a fair one. For now there is little reason to worry about the construction of proper procedures. If we are agreed that each party deserves a maximum amount of the cake compatible with a like amount for the other, then all we need do is divide the cake and give each party half. We are no longer worried about a fair division; we are worried instead about a just distribution. The focus on outcome now eliminates any reason to concern ourselves with procedure, and I want to say, the focus on justice now eliminates fairness concerns from the normative equation.

Interestingly, an associative morality permits us to retain the basic concerns of an interactive morality here and still arrive at a more intuitively fair distribution of the cake. Since fairness requires all parties to a bargain to work toward an equilibrium that maximally respects the interests of each party, the concern for the equal respect of interests is realized. This is required as a feature of the practice of bargaining, however, and not as a condition of equal concern for others qua persons. But of course, this also puts the parties to the distribution into a bargaining arrangement, and this means it is possible to identify any number of fair outcomes.

Perhaps one party to the division is particularly hungry, another does not like cake, another does not have a large appetite, and so forth. These factors may be introduced during the bargaining process as the parties attempt to arrive at what they mutually consider a fair distribution. And they may carry sufficient weight in the minds of the bargainers that they hit upon a distribution that is not fifty-fifty. Yet if they are agreed that the distribution crafted as a result of bargaining is acceptable, who are we to argue? A properly bargained distribution may not result in an equal distribution, but it would still be fair. And as should now be clear, there is no room left here for a moral objection to the distribution on the grounds that it really is not fair in the Kantian sense.

Now all this might show only that Rawls's example of perfect procedural justice actually better exemplifies an instance of what he calls pure procedural justice. There may be other instances, however, where the fairness of an outcome can be determined in advance of a fair bargain. But I am skeptical. The difficulty, as I see it, is that contested distributions cannot have proper outcomes knowable in advance and still raise fairness concerns. If they have known outcomes, it can only be because determinant desert claims are present that control our thinking about how a given distribution should be made. If so, then the concerns of justice indicate how things should be distributed and that is an end to the matter. An unjust distribution will be generically unfair, but otherwise, it will raise no pressing fairness concerns.[2] Fairness concerns do arise, however, if a distribution must be made in the absence of recognizable desert claims or if there is a desert tie. If such a distribution is to be made fairly, we must resort to either a bargaining process or a fairness mechanism. When recourse to bargaining is in order, the parties to the distribution must work amongst themselves to make a fair division, viz., a division hit upon as a result of an honest attempt at mutual accommodation.

If the parties bargain fairly, the interests of each party will be fully respected because this is part of what it means to bargain fairly, because this is what a bargainer owes to his fellow bargainers. If two individuals face the problem of dividing a cake both want, and if other things are considered equal, they may hit upon the strategy of dividing the cake in half. And they may decide that the best way to guard against subtle defection is to have one cut the cake and the other choose the first piece. Of course, they may also decide upon an all-or-nothing strategy and flip a coin. If they are so agreed, this too would yield a fair outcome.

This brings me to Rawls's notion of imperfect procedural justice which he illustrates by means of the example of a criminal trial. He says, "The desired outcome is that the defendant should be declared guilty if and only if he has committed the offense with which he is charged. The trial procedure is framed to search for and to establish the truth in this regard. But it seems impossible to design the legal rules so that they always lead to the correct result" (1971: p. 85).

The use of this example, however, is rather unfortunate. Rawls apparently fails to appreciate the type of "desired outcome" that is appropriate for a criminal trial, at least under American law. Nor is it quite right to say that the law of criminal procedure is designed to discover truth about guilt or innocence. To illustrate, imagine that A has brought about B's death in a manner suggestive of murder and that the police learn of this by means of what a constitutional lawyer would call an unreasonable search. Since it looks like A has committed the offense with which he has been charged, Rawls would apparently say that the desired outcome is a declaration of guilt. But the actual determination of legal guilt in a criminal proceeding depends upon a strict adherence to process and results only as an outcome of that process.

In American law, for example, the prosecution must not only prove guilt beyond a reasonable doubt; it must also do so by adhering to the rules of criminal prosecution. If the rules are not followed, if the state acts unfairly by breaking the rules of prosecution, then conviction is not justified. Even if the defendant is factually guilty (i.e., A really did murder B), the failure to follow the proper rules of adjudication means that the a guilty verdict would be unfair. The ideal of adversarial justice, including the presumption of innocence and the notion of legal guilt, sets the telos of the practice of criminal justice in the United States and controls thinking about the fairness of a trial. Moreover, these fairness concerns inform our ideas about the justness of the prosecutorial outcome. Punishment for criminal wrongdoing is deserved only if criminal responsibility is established as the result of a fair trial.

In this sense, trials resemble athletic competitions. The aim of the trial process is to determine criminal responsibility, just as the aim of an athletic contest is to determine athletic excellence of some sort. But these determinations can only be made by means of the practices themselves. We might say that the ideal end of the trial process is to convict the guilty and acquit the innocent; just as we might say that the ideal end of an athletic contest is to have the best competitor win. But we do not know who the best competitor is until we play the game; just as we do not know if a person is legally guilty of a crime until we have a trial. So, the example Rawls uses to illustrate imperfect procedural justice also appears to reduce to something like a case of pure procedural justice. Once again, there may be other contested practices that would better exemplify imperfect procedural justice. But I am still skeptical, and for the same reasons that led me to question our ability to make sense of perfect procedural justice.

So much then for efforts to support the notion of Kantian fairness by claiming that some distributive situations have antecedently determinate results. If such results are evident, they must be the product of relevant desert considerations and this transforms a concern for process into a concern for doing justice. But if distributions must be made in the absence of applicable desert considerations, then recourse must be had to those purposive practices customarily understood to serve such a need. Now the concerns of justice yield to considerations of fairness and a focus on the process by which distributions are determined.

Notes

1. Things might be different if B was in the business of providing a service that A happens to need under the circumstances. But we are not accustomed to paying lifeguards for their rescues; public safety is arguably a need that we provide one another as a condition of what Walzer calls communal provision (Walzer, 1983: pp. 68-74).

2. Since philosophers frequently use the notion of Kantian fairness as a synonym for justice, we could say that an unjust distribution is an unfair distribution in the Kantian sense. Once again, there is nothing wrong with speaking this way, provided we are clear on the distinction between Kantian fairness and our more traditional moral notion of fairness.

Chapter Nine

Fairness and Virtue

So far my inquiry into the nature of fairness has focused primarily upon the notions of fair play, fair bargaining and dealing, fair distributions, and the fairness of rules and procedures. Such concerns arise within the context of purposive social practices to which fellow cooperators must remain faithful if things are to go as they should. Accordingly, the demands of fairness are important for their smooth operation. And this is some indication that the notion of fairness belongs to an associative morality--a moral perspective which calls attention to the normative importance of the responsibilities we have as associated beings, or as beings linked to one another by virtue of a shared involvement in certain cooperative ventures.

I want now to bring the discussion to a conclusion by exploring two further issues. The first might be put in the form of an objection to my general argument. Thinking of fairness in terms of fidelity to purposive social practices will seem incomplete, and hence inadequate, if it is possible to worry about the fairness of certain practices themselves. If it makes sense to ask whether a practice itself is fair, and not simply whether its procedures or rules are fair, we will need to see if this can be explained in terms of the account of fairness presented above. I think there are occasions when it is both possible and appropriate to ask about the fairness of certain purposive practices in this manner, and so there is more explaining to do.

Second, we often speak of fairness as an attribute of individuals, or as a type of virtue. More specifically, we occasionally praise people for being fairminded. Virtues, of course, are the building blocks of a good person. They are also "functional" in an important sense. The virtuous person is a good associative being, for virtues promote and support the well-being of the larger community to which the virtuous person belongs. It seems plausible, then, to think of fairmindedness as a virtue within the context provided by an associative morality. This point needs to be developed more fully, however, and this also leaves me with more explaining to do.

The Fairness of Social Practices

Is it possible to question the fairness of social practices themselves? Concern over the fairness of a practice is distinguishable from concern about the fairness of its procedures or the fairness of its participants. An election is unfair, i.e., it has an unfair outcome, if one candidate finds a way to get enough corpses to vote for him to overcome the winning margin his opponent has among the living, eligible voters who went to the polls. But an election may also be unfair if its procedures do not correspond with the democratic ideals that inspire a commitment to electoral politics. Someone might think an election unfair, for example, if it is not governed by the principle of one person, one vote. Others might think this principle itself is unfair and, like John Stuart Mill, prefer an electoral system with weighted votes. These matters raise fairness concerns because they ask us to consider what procedures and structures are appropriate to, or required by, the telos of the practice itself. That is, they introduce competing views about the material element of a fair election.

We reach another level of concern, however, when we ask whether elections themselves are really fair. Democratic polities characteristically rely upon elections in order to transfer political power. So, to ask whether elections themselves are fair is to ask if they provide an acceptable method for the transference of this power. This issue raises questions, not about the way elections operate in a particular polity, but about whether elections should be used at all when it comes to transferring political power. It raises the possibility that there may be something wrong or corrupt about the practice itself that makes it undesirable in itself and that the infirmity in question is properly understandable in terms of fairness.

We may claim a practice is generically unfair, of course, if we have reason to dislike it, or if we think it suffers from any number of possible ills. But this is not what concerns me at present. I want to ask if it makes sense to think that social practices, or at least some social practices, can suffer from a more specific infirmity identified by the notion of fairness.

Many of the purposive social practices that house fairness concerns cannot themselves be critiqued as fair or unfair. It makes little sense, for example, to ask if baseball is fair or not. We can ask if a particular baseball game was played fairly, and when we do, we ask about whether the game was played and officiated in a manner faithful to the game's telos. We can also ask, as we have seen, whether a particular rule is fair or not, and when we do, we want to know whether the rule is appropriate given the purpose of the activity. But it sounds strange to ask whether baseball--the game--is fair. Baseball--the game--is neither fair nor unfair; it is just a game people play and watch--a source of amusement and entertainment surrounding a particular test of skill and excellence--and that is an end to the matter. If a game is brutal, if it permits or requires violence and even cruelty, we may think, from the standpoint of an interactive morality, that the game is immoral. But we would still not say that it is unfair, or even that it is unjust. Though its enthusiasts may not see our point, we condemn it as best we can when we say it is violent or brutal.

Still there do seem to be situations where it makes sense to ask about the fairness of some practice. Suppose, for example, we question the fairness of the electoral process or perhaps the system of adversarial justice. Should we do so, we are asking about whether these practices establish a fair way to do certain things, viz., transfer political power or affix criminal liability. Such questions bring to the fore the larger social implications of these practices, and in doing so, they encourage us to evaluate our use of them in terms of the basic social ideals and norms to which we are committed as a community. In the absence of these more basic ideals, inquiring into the fairness of practices that establish certain ways of doing things would be pointless. But because communities do have such ideals, it makes sense to ask if the social practices they use in order to meet socially necessary jobs and provide socially useful functions are faithful to the ideals that govern thinking about how things in the community should go. That is, it makes sense to ask if these practices are fair.

In this regard, we can even ask if baseball is fair. If we do, we are not asking about the game itself; for as we have seen, the game itself is neither fair nor unfair. But even though it is just a game, it may have much broader social implications. And these may trigger a concern for the fairness of the game as it manifests itself in the community. We might wonder, for example, if it is fair to permit successful baseball players to realize tremendous financial success by showcasing their skills, even if the viewing audience pays willingly for the opportunity to watch the players play.

The social practices most likely to give rise to this type of fairness concern generally establish specific ways of managing certain social tasks, or meeting societal needs. Community members have a right to expect that the tasks performed, or the needs met, will be accomplished in a manner faithful to, if not specifically informed by, community norms. The democratic process will qualify as fair, then, in polities that value some form of citizen input into the process by which political power is transferred, or insist that the governors be answerable, in some fashion, to the governed.

This brings a concern for the fairness of social practices close to the issue of social justice. If we think that social justice is chiefly concerned with the structure and function of those practices that serve the collective needs of the community, a concern for the fairness of these practices will go to the heart of social justice. The norms that articulate the ideal of justice for the community will then provide the normative standard with which to measure the fairness of these practices. And conversely, conclusions about their fairness will shed light on the justness of the community. A particular social practice is fair, this is to say, if it is faithful to the ends and ideals that shape the normative convictions of the community with regard to civil association. So, if the practices of a community qualify as fair in this way, they also meet the standards of social justice that inform the telos of the community.

But perhaps the issue of social justice goes deeper than this. Perhaps social justice is also concerned with the nature of the social norms that prevail in the state. If so, then a state can be unjust if its dominant norms and fundamental ideals are morally offensive. Yet, if social practices faithfully implement these ideals, repugnant though they might be, the state might qualify as unjust but the practices by means of which it implements its ideals and performs socially necessary tasks could not be considered unfair. There is simply no defection from its governing ideals or telos in evidence here. This is obviously small solace for those who consider the state unjust, but it also illustrates that the concerns of social justice are not simply conterminous with the fairness of its institutions and practices.

If we consider the issue from the perspective provided by an associative moral theory, however, there is more that should be said at this point. An associative morality supposes that individuals can be, and generally are, linked to one another in practices that give meaning and direction to their lives. One's sense of self and one's sense of purpose and meaning in life are largely, if not entirely, given by one's associative attachments (Cf. MacIntyre, 1988: pp. 124-46; Taylor, 1985: pp. 248-88). Individuals find meaning and purpose by participating in their communities and by contributing to the social units with which they are identified and to which they belong. But this view of civil life is also easily, and properly reversible. By participating in the community and contributing to its social life, citizens serve one another's needs and contribute to each other's well being. Put in more general terms, it is both appropriate and desirable to say that the community exists to serve the needs of its citizenry. This is its guiding purpose; this is its *raison d'être*.

Political association, then, is purposive in much the way that an athletic contest is purposive. Athletic contests permit individuals to come together for the purpose of testing their talents and abilities in a particular manner. Athletes cannot test their skills alone or in isolation, although in some instances they can practice and develop their abilities in this manner. But to test and employ these skills, they need one another's company, and they need the context provided by the game or event. So they must work together or not at all. Similarly, political association involves persons coming together for purposes of mutual support, common defense, and increased provision, among other things. The support, defense, and provision made available through political association cannot be achieved by individuals acting independently, or at least it cannot be achieved as fully as possible and probably as fully as one would like. So, to realize these goals and meet these needs, people must again work together.

Now, under an associative morality, the norms and ideals that direct a community of fellow cooperators should reflect and support the telos of the community. If the norms in question favor some and victimize others, the unit in question fails to qualify as a community. Instead, it becomes a predatory arrangement where some victimize, exploit, and denigrate others for their own advantage. Here there are no fellow cooperators; there are only oppressors and oppressed. States in which the rule of law works as a mechanism of oppression are not polities, or communities, in an important sense. For polities, as a type of community, need to be faithful to the telos of political association, and this is fixed by our understanding of why it is reasonable for persons to come together and form such associations in the first place.

So, an associative morality requires us to condemn states, like Nazi Germany, as unjust because of the deep corruption in the ideals that forge its political morality. Needless to say, these ideals may be objectionable from the moral vantage point supplied by the morality of happiness and an interactive morality as well. But we need not resort to one of these moral theories to condemn such states. However, from the standpoint of an associative morality, it would not do to conflate fairness and social justice at this point. Because political association is purposive, states that fail to honor the purposes which underlie it are properly condemned as unjust. This would include, for example, those states whose political norms permit or even require the oppression of groups or individuals residing within their borders. Fairness concerns, on the other hand, arise only within practices bounded by and dedicated to appropriate purposes. For fairness to be an issue, we must first have a community of fellow cooperators. An unjust state is hardly such a community; it fails to meet the basic associative requirements of a political community or polity. Consequently, we do not, and should not, conceptualize the injustice associated with a predatory state as a type of unfairness. There is no betrayal here because there is no real common association. It is both possible and necessary, then, to speak of an unjust state from the point of view provided by an associative morality without also thinking that states are unjust because they are unfair.

Within reasonably just polities, however, the unfairness of a practice can be a mark of social injustice, and from the standpoint of an associative morality, it is worth emphasizing this point. Consider, for example, the practice of slavery in America's antebellum south. Based upon the fundamental telos of political association, this practice was unjust, and if it turned out that the practice was justified by the basic norms and fundamental ideals of the American polity, the United States would be properly condemned as an unjust state. But in fact the practice seems quite inconsistent with American ideals about liberty and equality, and even during its day slavery in American was considered by a great many Americans, particularly in the north, to be grossly inconsistent with America's political ideals.

Let us suppose this was in fact the case (Cf. Hartz, 1955: pp. 145-84). That is, let us suppose the practice was unfaithful to the Lockean liberal ideals which largely influence the norms of American political culture and which were widely embraced (at some level of generality) throughout the American polity, including the antebellum south, at the time. (I am, to be sure, aware that this is a controversial assumption.) If we suppose further that these ideals align rather nicely with the general telos of political association (not a horribly unreasonable assumption), it is possible to think of antebellum America as a polity and not an unjust state. But the practice of slavery also qualifies as unfair because it is inconsistent with these ideals, and this unfairness is, in turn, a material element of the notion of social injustice. This critique of the unfairness of a practice like slavery in a state that qualifies as a polity matters, moreover, because it explains why slavery in a polity is unjust. It is unjust, that is, because it is unfair, because a part of the population of the community is treated in a manner inconsistent with the ideals that set the standards for how fellow cooperators are to treat one another. This seems a particularly vicious form of political betrayal.

There is an indication, in all this, of the power and currency of thinking of the norms and ideals of political association in the terms supplied by an associative morality. Consider, for example, two ways a defender of the practice of slavery in the antebellum south might attempt to deflect the claim that slavery is unjust because unfair. He might argue that the African-Americans forced to endure the status of slavery were not rightfully regarded as persons, or he might claim that they were not rightfully regarded as part of the community. Both of these claims have been used to justify or defend social practices (as well as interpersonal activities) that serve the purpose of isolating, enslaving, or marginalizing certain elements of the population (See e.g., Higham, 1955). The first move is consonant with an interactive morality; we are exempted from treating others with equal concern if the "others" in question fail to qualify as others, i.e., as persons. But of course, it also works to escape the force of an associative morality; for if the other is not a person, he or she cannot be a fellow cooperator either.

The second move, however, is exculpable only from the standpoint of an associative morality. We need not treat outsiders fairly, the argument goes, because they are not a part of our community; thus, they fail to qualify as fellow cooperators. They are invaders, perhaps; threats to our way of life. Or they are too immature, too underdeveloped, to qualify as members of our community. The sounds of xenophobia are many and all seem sadly familiar. They are attempts to exclude, and by so doing, to defeat the demands of an associative morality. When it comes to political association, they are often justifications, or rationalizations for unfairness, and their injustice lies in this fact. Where an interactive morality condemns because of the inappropriate treatment of other persons, an associative morality condemns because of the failure to treat all of us as a part of us.

The sounds of xenophobia tend to ring hollow, however, because just polities possess normative standards that determine who belongs to the polity and who does not, who is properly a member and who is not. And these standards go some distance toward exposing xenophobia for what it really is. It would, I suspect, be a mistake to deny that American slavery was an abomination because it is so disparately wrong to treat a human being as chattel, but I also don't think that this gets all the way to the injustice of slavery in America. We begin to get all the way when we appreciate what is wrong with the claim that African-Americans were not part of the community. For under the ideals of American political culture, they were indeed a part of the community; they did indeed qualify as fellow cooperators.

This conclusion seems unavoidable if we take seriously the liberal ideals of liberty and equality, as well as the mere fact of African-American presence in, and contributions to, their social environment. While legislative exclusion might set a legal standard for thinking about community membership, it cannot override the ideals that presumably govern community reflection on who belongs and who does not.

If this is the fact that stings the most from a moral point of view, if it is the betrayal of certain Americans by other Americans that goes to the heart of the injustice of slavery in America, then there is something to be said for the standards of an associative morality. Correspondingly, if the perspective supplied by an associative morality seems a more intuitively plausible account of the moral evil identified with social practices like slavery in the antebellum south, then we have reason to think that the evaluation of the fairness or unfairness of such social practices can shed considerable light on the relative justness of a polity.

Fairmindedness

We sometimes ascribe fairness to persons as such and not simply to their actions. We do so, for example, when we praise a person for being fairminded. As an attribute of persons, fairness is best regarded as a virtue like courage or temperance. While a fair person is not necessarily also a good person, a fairminded individual is virtuous in at least this one way, and this is a step in the direction of goodness. But then, how should we describe or understand the virtue of being fairminded?

Virtues are indicators of sociability. Virtuous individuals display character traits that are important to, if not necessary for, the well-being of the community. Courage, for example is classically considered to be an important virtue because the courageous make good warriors and defenders of the community. The cultivation of the virtues, then, is a matter of some importance according to an associative morality. The virtues make a fellow cooperator a more reliable and dedicated member of the community, or a more trustworthy participant in some purposive practice.

As we have seen, purposive practices go better if their participants are dedicated to their ends and ideals. This, I have argued, is what fairness demands. Correspondingly, the fairminded individual is one who is faithful to the spirit of the social practice in which she or he is a participant. This involves a commitment to others, to be sure, but it is a particular type of commitment. It is a commitment to certain specifiable others--one's fellow cooperators--to adhere to certain, again specifiable, rules, procedures, policies, or expectations--namely, the rules and expectations, etc., associated with the telos of the practice in question.

Fairmindedness, in short, displays the virtue of a cooperative spirit. Fairness, like honesty, trust, and perhaps generosity, is a fundamental virtue of association. Fairminded individuals will want to do their share, to play and bargain fairly, and so on because they understand this to be required by the associative character of their particular involvement with certain others. The fairminded person sees herself first and foremost as a fellow associate and she participates accordingly in those purposive social enterprises to which she belongs. No doubt fairminded individuals understand that they have an obligation to adhere to the rules and procedures of the practices in which they participate, and no doubt they appreciate the fact that this obligation is based upon their associative involvement with specific others--this is something of what it means to see oneself as a fellow cooperator. But the focus on obligation is rather misleading when it comes to a consideration of fairmindedness. For the fairminded individual cooperates as a matter of course, and because she understands the implications of her role as a fellow cooperator. One wants to say here that the fairminded individual cooperates naturally, so to speak, or perhaps habitually, and not out of some grudging sense of obligation.

Consequently, it is rather misleading to say that a fairminded person is simply one who plays, trades, bargains, deals, or participates fairly. It is possible to act or play fairly without being fairminded. Someone might play fairly because she is worried that she might get caught cheating and feel embarrassed, or someone might play fairly because she knows she can probably win without cheating. These are instances of fair play, but not of fairmindedness. The fairminded person plays fairly because this is the thing to do, and in playing or acting fairly, the fairminded person simply displays her fairmindedness.

Fairminded individuals may fall short of being good persons. They may not show much care, or demonstrate much concern for fellow associates. A fairminded person can play a game fairly, for example, and still play rudely, even cruelly. Someone who is fairminded may think nothing of embarrassing her opponent and might even choose to play aggressively against a weaker opponent in order to humiliate her. We would not expect this of a good person, but nothing here is inconsistent with being faithful to the purpose and ideals of the competition simply as a matter of course. Nor need fairminded individuals hold their fellow cooperators in high regard or respect them as persons. In fact, they may have great personal disdain for their opponents, bargaining partners, neighbors, or fellow citizens. Fairminded individuals will remain steadfast in their commitment to the practice in which they are involved because they see themselves as fellow cooperators and not because of any particular regard they may happen to have for their fellow cooperators.

Fairness, then, seems best understood as a fundamental virtue of sociability. Social life will surely go better if people are fairminded, but it goes better even if people must struggle to be fair and against the inclination to put themselves first and ignore or disregard their social responsibilities. Fairness matters because we generally need to pull together, to work together, and to struggle together to achieve the ends of those purposive practices to which we happen to belong, and which might well be integral to the well-being of the participants themselves. It demands that we do our part and keep faith with the associative activities we happen to be in, either as a matter of choice or fate. As a virtue, it reminds us that we are linked to certain others regardless of the temptation to think that we are in conflict with them. It builds a sense of sociability just where it often seems most needed, at the point where conflict and competition become potentially destructive of the deeper fact of necessary cooperation.

As a social virtue, fairness minimizes the appearance of social distance between fellow cooperators and reduces the inclination to see others, in Marx's protean phrase, as alien beings. It does so, moreover, under circumstances where people may have independent reasons to dislike or disregard others. Because it emphasizes the need for cooperation, because it encourages us to recognize our social attachments even to those we may dislike, it is also a political virtue of great importance. It supports the recognition of associative identity within the larger social context of pluralism and group difference. Fairness does not unite fellow participants in a social practice as tightly as other virtues of sociability like, say, friendship or love. But this is hardly a reason for criticism. Not all purposive practices will display the solidarity or comprehensiveness of identification that is on display in a family or fraternal organization. Fairness is not much of a virtue where love or brotherhood are (or are supposed to be) at work. But these virtues matter only in the most intimate of associative linkages and are hardly appropriate for the welter of purposive practices that are composed of strangers with little or nothing else in common besides their mutual participation. Fairness matters most in these contexts. It is here that people are most likely to overlook or disregard the implications of their associative identifications, and it is here that the norm of fairness operates to hold them to their associative responsibilities.

By way of illustration, consider the game of American football. Imagine two teams that have never played before coming together for a game. Players on these teams may not know their adversaries, though if they have scouted their opponent they will know of them. And when the game begins, they confront unrecognizable strangers--individuals hidden from view by pads and helmets. Beings barely recognizable as human draw up in front of them and prepare to lunge at them with all the power and strength they can muster. Yet even though these opponents seem like threatening strangers, the players will know one important thing: They are fellow cooperators dedicated to the same game to which they are committed. Regardless of whatever else separates them, both teams, we can suppose, are devoted to the game, and the contest is both possible and important for this reason.

A second and arguably more important illustration of the virtue of fairness is provided by political association. Fairness is perhaps the first virtue of citizenship and this is reason to cultivate fairmindedness in the citizenry. As fellow cooperators in a common polity, we are not asked to like our fellow citizens, let alone to love them, but we are asked, and should be asked, to get along with them. As citizens, we owe it to our fellow cooperators to be faithful to the ideals of political association that both define and inspire the polity as a purposive practice. This might be regarded as the political manifestation of fair play, and it requires citizens to conduct themselves in the manner commonly understood to guarantee that life in the polity will go well or at least reasonably well under the circumstances. In her capacity as citizen, the fairminded person will recognize an obligation to obey the law, to support and promote the political practices and institutions of the polity, to contribute her share to the common defense of the polity, and so forth. While normative pluralism might be a common feature of many contemporary polities, the demands of an associative morality look through, or rather beyond, these basic differences and make possible *civil* association in the presence of otherwise extraordinary diversity.

Fairness as a virtue might be considered the social glue that holds associations together in the face of the forces that work to pull them apart. The more fairmindedness is cultivated in a community, the more secure community members may feel about their future. Yet fairness is only one brand of conceptual glue that secures associative identification within the community. There are others, and the full articulation of an associative moral theory is necessary in order to appreciate the way moral norms support and sustain those associative attachments that define and direct the lives of fellow cooperators.

At times, however, we must face a problem that will surely trouble fairminded individuals. What should a fairminded person do when her fellow cooperators begin to defect from a social practice in large numbers. Mass defections, at some point, will throw the integrity of the practice into doubt. Imagine, for example, that people seeking tickets to the theater refuse to queue up and instead push forward and crowd around the ticket booth. At what point does it no longer make sense for a fairminded person to remain steadfast to the telos of the practice in which he participates? At what point, to put the question differently, is there no longer a practice to continue?

These are important questions. To repeat a point that bears repeating, if defections are so great that the purpose served by the practice is defeated, there is no longer any reason to continue to participate. But defection is rarely this extreme. If the practice matters to its participants, they will, at some point, refuse to defect. And fairminded individuals will be inclined to play or participate fairly until it is evident that there is little left of the practice itself. This may seem irrational to some. If others are defecting, and if defection will guarantee the realization of one's personal interest without great cost, then rationality might counsel in favor of defection. But when such defections become commonplace, when the social glue fairness provides is weakened and fairmindedness begins to atrophy, the associative attachments that matter deeply to people are also endangered.

The best defense against such a situation is the continued cultivation of fairmindedness, and in the process it can do no harm to point out that fairness works to the advantage of social beings who live with others and not simply in the company of others. So, there is reason to remain steadfast to a purposive practice even when large numbers of others defect. This keeps the virtue of fairness alive, and as associative beings we have reason to want to see this happen. Virtues, after all, serve a purpose; from a moral point of view, they have important functions. This is not reason, however, to think that a defense of fairmindedness reduces to a utilitarian argument. It may be that we will be happier if we live in a community where fairmindedness is encouraged and cultivated. Because we are associative beings, we should expect as much. But fairmindedness qualifies as a moral virtue because we are associative beings and because it is so important to the process of association characteristic of human *being*, and hence of *being* human.

Fairness as an End

I have been concerned here to explore the notion of fairness as an aspect of our moral lives. The effort to make sense of some commonplace material fairness concerns led me to reject several of the most familiar theoretical accounts of fairness in favor of a description of the formal element of fairness as fidelity to purposive social practice. To make sense of this, in turn, I argued that it is necessary to see the notion of fairness as a component of an associative moral theory. As a result, my argument distances the ordinary moral notion of fairness from the technical sense the term is often given by philosophers working within the tradition of an interactive morality (or from Kantian fairness). I have argued that fairness, as an ordinary moral notion that figures prominently in the lives of persons wanting to live worthwhile moral lives, cannot be readily or properly understood from the perspective supplied by such a view of morality.

An adequate understanding of fairness as a moral notion, then, requires a shift in perspective. We cannot begin to appreciate the moral significance fairness has for us unless we see ourselves not as independent and detached moral units, but as associative beings interlocked with others in a myriad of different practices. Many of these have some end, some telos, or some set of ideals and principles to which we must remain faithful in order for things to go as we think they should. It is not, however, the desire to see the practice go as it should that explains why we should be fair. Instead, we should be fair because this is our responsibility as a fellow cooperator. If fairness mattered only as long as the practice proceeds as it ideally should, the responsibility to be fair would be removed at the first sign of defection.

Yet wording is tricky here and precision is of great importance. It is not quite right to say that we should be fair because this is our responsibility as associative beings. More properly, fairness *is* our responsibility by virtue of the associative attachments that we have. This puts things in proper perspective; or rather, this is the way we must understand fairness as a moral notion. That is, this is how we must see fairness given the perspective supplied by an associative morality. For the need to be fair, and the complementary need to cultivate the virtue of fairmindedness, becomes apparent once we are reminded of the associative nature of our lives--once we see ourselves as social beings, as beings who engage actively with others in the adventures of a shared life.

Bibliography

Arneson, Richard (1982). "The Principle of Fairness and Free Rider Problems." *Ethics* 92: 616-13.

Barry, Brian (1965). *Political Argument*. London: Routledge & Kegan Paul.

——— (1989). *Theories of Justice*. Berkeley: University of California Press.

Berger, Peter (1970). "On the Obsolescence of the Concept of Honor." *European Journal of Sociology* 11: 339-47.

Black, Max (1962). *Model and Metaphors*. Ithaca, N.Y.: Cornell University Press.

Bosanquet, Bernard (1951). *The Philosophical Theory of the State*. London: Macmillan.

Bourdieu, Pierre (1990). *The Logic of Practice*. Stanford, Calif.: Stanford University Press.

——— (1990). *In Other Words*. Stanford, Calif.: Stanford University Press.

Brams, Steven and Taylor, Alan (1996). *Fair Division*. Cambridge: Cambridge University Press.

Brandt, Richard B. (1965). "The Concepts of Obligation and Duty." *Mind* 73: 374-93.

Broad, C.D. (1916). "On the Function of False Hypothesis in Ethics." *International Journal of Ethics* 26: 377-97.

——— (1948). *Five Types of Ethical Theories*. London: Kegan Paul, Trench, Trubner.

Broome, John (1991). "Fairness." *Proceedings of the Aristotelian Society* 91: 87-101.

——— (1994). "Fairness Versus Doing the Most Good." *Hastings Center Report* 24: 36-39.

Byron, Michael, "Rationality is Not Fair." *Analysis* 55: 252-60.

Carpenter, David (1994). "Elements of Accounting Ethics: The Notion of Fairness." *Business Professional Ethics Journal* 13: 57-77.

Carr, Craig L. (1981). "The Concept of Formal Justice." *Philosophical Studies* 39: 211-26.

——— (1988). "Coercion and Freedom." *American Philosophical Quarterly* 25: 59-67.

——— (1990). "Tacit Consent." *Public Affairs Quarterly* 4: 335-45.

Cote, Elizabeth (1989). *Learn The Value of Fairness*. Vero Beach, Fl.: Rourke Enterprises.

Darwall, Stephen (1983). *Impartial Reason*. Ithaca, N.Y.: Cornell University Press.

Day, J.P. (1977). "Fairness and Fortune." *Ratio* 19: 70-84.

Downie, R.S., and Telfer, Elizabeth (1970). *Respect for Persons*. New York: Shocken.

Elster, Jon (1989). *The Cement of Society*. Cambridge: Cambridge University Press.

Feinberg, Joel (1970). *Doing and Deserving*. Princeton, N.J.: Princeton University Press.

——— (1984). *Harm to Others: The Moral Limits of the Criminal Law, Volume One*. Oxford: Oxford University Press.

——— (1988). *Harmless Wrongdoing: The Moral Limits of the Criminal Law, Volume Four*. Oxford: Oxford University Press.

Frankena, William (1962). "The Concept of Social Justice." In Richard Brandt (ed.), *Social Justice*. Englewood Cliffs, N.J.: Prentice-Hall.

Friedman, Marilyn (1991). "The Practice of Partiality." *Ethics* 101: 818-35.

Gauthier, David (1986). *Morals by Agreement*. Oxford: Clarendon.

Gewirth, Alan (1978). *Reason and Morality*. Chicago: University of Chicago Press.

Giddens, Anthony (1979). *Central Problems in Social Theory*. Berkeley: University of California Press.

Greenawalt, Kent (1987). *Conflicts of Law and Morality*. New York: Oxford University Press.

Griffin, James (1985). "Some Problems of Fairness." *Ethics* 96: 100-18.

Haksar, Vinit (1976). "Coercive Proposals (Rawls and Gandhi)." *Political Theory* 4: 65-79.

Hart, H.L.A. (1955). "Are There Any Natural Rights." *Philosophical Review* 64: 175-91.

——— (1961). *The Concept of Law*. Oxford: Oxford University Press.

Hartz, Louis (1955). *The Liberal Tradition in America*. New York: Harcourt, Brace & World.

Held, Virginia (1972). "Coercion and Coercive Offers." In J.R. Pennock and J.W. Chapman (eds.), *Coercion*. Chicago: Atherton.

Higham, John (1955). *Strangers in the Land*. New Brunswick, N.J.: Rutgers University Press.

Hinton, J.M. (1990). "Knowing and Valuing Fairness." *Philosophy* 65: 271-96.

Kamooneh, K. (1987). "Justice as Fairness or as Equality." *Journal of Value Inquiry* 21: 65-71.

Kant, Immanuel (1969). *Foundations of the Metaphysics of Morals*. R.P. Wolff (ed.). Indianapolis: Bobbs-Merrill.

Katzner, Louis L. (1971). "Presumptive and Nonpresumptive Principles of Formal Justice." *Ethics* 81: 253-58.

Klosko, George (1992). *The Principle of Fairness and Political Obligation*. Lanham, MD.: Rowman & Littlefield.

Kovesi, Julius (1967). *Moral Notions*. London: Routledge & Kegan Paul.

Ladd, John (1970). "Legal and Moral Obligation." In J.R. Pennock and J.W. Chapman (eds.), *Political and Legal Obligation*. New York: Atherton.

——— (1998). "The Idea of Community, an Ethical Exploration, Part I: The Search for an Elusive Concept." *The Journal of Value Inquiry* 32: 5-24.

Lyons, David (1965). *Forms and Limits of Utilitarianism*. Oxford: Oxford University Press.

Lyotard, Jean-François (1984). *The Postmodern Condition*. Minneapolis: University of Minnesota Press.

Lyotard, Jean François, and Thébaud, Jean-Loup (1985). *Just Gaming*. Minneapolis: University of Minnesota Press.

MacIntyre, Alasdair (1981). *After Virtue*. Notre Dame, Ind.: University of Notre Dame Press.

——— (1988). *Whose Justice? Which Rationality?* Notre Dame, Ind.: University of Notre Dame Press.

Martin, Mike W. (1993). "What's Fair in Love." *Southern Journal of Philosophy* 31: 393-407.

Nagel, Thomas (1970). *The Possibility of Altruism*. Oxford: Clarendon.

——— (1986). *The View from Nowhere*. New York: Oxford University Press.

——— (1991). *Equality and Rationality*. Oxford: Oxford University Press.

Nozick, Robert (1969). "Coercion." In S. Morgenbesser, P. Suppes, and M. White (eds.), *Philosophy, Science, and Method: Essays in Honor of Ernest Nagel*. New York: St. Martin's.

——— (1974). *Anarchy, State, and Utopia*. New York: Basic Books.

Oakeshott, Michael (1975). *On Human Conduct*. Oxford: Clarendon.

Perelman, Chaim (1963). *The Idea of Justice and the Problem of Argument*. London: Routledge & Kegan Paul.

Pieper, A. (1991). "Fairness as an Ethical Principle." *Deutsche Zeitschrift Für Philosophie* 39: 890-99.

Raiffa, Howard (1982). *The Art and Science of Negotiation*. Cambridge: Belknap Press of Harvard University Press.

Raphael, D.D. (1955). *Moral Judgment*. London: Allen & Unwin.

Rawls, John (1958). "Justice as Fairness." *Philosophical Review* 67: 164-94.

——— (1971). *A Theory of Justice*. Cambridge: Belknap Press of Harvard University Press.

Sachs, David (1995). "Notes on Unfairly Gaining More: 'Pleonexia.'" In Rosalind Hursthouse (ed.), *Virtues and Reasons*. Oxford: Clarendon.

Sandel, Michael (1982). *Liberalism and the Limits of Justice*. Cambridge: Cambridge University Press.

Schatzki, Theodore (1996). *Social Practices*. Cambridge: Cambridge University Press.

Schauer, Frederick (1991). *Playing By the Rules*. Oxford: Clarendon.

Sher, George (1980). "What Makes a Lottery Fair?" *Noûs* 14: 203-15.

______ (1987). *Desert*. Princeton, N.J.: Princeton University Press.

Sidgwick, Henry (1919). *The Elements of Politics* (4th ed.). London: Macmillan.

——— (1966). *The Methods of Ethics* (7th ed.). New York: Dover.

Simmons, A. John (1979). "The Principle of Fair Play." *Philosophy and Public Affairs* 8: 307-37.

——— (1979). *Moral Principles and Political Obligations*. Princeton, N.J.: Princeton University Press.

Sullivan, Daniel (1975). "Rules, Fairness, and Formal Justice." *Ethics* 85: 322-331.

Szaniawski, Klemens (1991). "On Fair Distribution of Indivisible Goods." In Peter Geach (ed.), *Logic and Ethics*. Boston: Kluwer.

Taylor, Charles (1985). "Interpretation and the Sciences of Man." In Charles Taylor, *Philosophical Papers 2*. Cambridge: Cambridge University Press.

Wallace, R. Jay (1994). *Responsibility and the Moral Sentiments*. Cambridge: Harvard University Press.

Walzer, Michael (1983). *Spheres of Justice*. New York: Basic Books.

Wertheimer, Alan (1996). *Exploitation*. Princeton, N.J.: Princeton University Press.

Williams, Bernard (1967). "The Idea of Equality." In Peter Laslett and W.G. Runciman (eds.), *Philosophy, Politics, and Society* (2nd series). Oxford: Basil Blackwell.

——— (1981). *Moral Luck*. Cambridge: Cambridge University Press.

Winch, Peter (1958). *The Idea of a Social Science and its Relation to Philosophy*. London: Routledge & Kegan Paul.

Wittgenstein, Ludwig (1953). *Philosophical Investigations*. New York: Macmillan.

Wolff, Jonathan (1995). "Political Obligation, Fairness and Independence." *Ratio* 8: 87-99.

——— (1998). "Fairness, Respect, and The Egalitarian Ethos." *Philosophy and Public Affairs* 27: 97-122.

Index